MW01277345

PENGUIN BOOKS

CONQUER
Your Email
OVERLOAD

Debbie Mayo-Smith is a top ranking international motivational business speaker and author.

Acclaimed as a leading expert in Internet and email marketing, Debbie was one of the first in Australasia to understand the benefits, practical uses as well as pitfalls of this medium. Her speciality is helping individuals improve their personal productivity and business profitability.

After earning a Double Honours Bachelor of Science in Economics and Geography from the Southern Connecticut State University, USA, Debbie worked on Wall Street as a Market Analyst. A native New Yorker, Debbie moved to New Zealand where she now lives with husband Steve, and their six children.

Other books written by Debbie Mayo-Smith are available on www.debbiespeaks.co.nz or ask for them at your local bookshop:

Successful Email Marketing - Your Complete 'How-To' Guide

Superb Tips and Tricks for Managing Your Customer Information

Professional Online Newsletters and Emails - Exactly How To Create Your Own

http://www.debbiespeaks.co.nz/books.htm

CONQUER
Your Email
OVERLOAD

SUPERB TIPS AND TRICKS FOR BUSY PEOPLE

Debbie Mayo-Smith

PENGUIN BOOKS

PENGUIN BOOKS
Published by the Penguin Group
Penguin Group (NZ), cnr Airborne and Rosedale Roads, Albany,
Auckland 1310, New Zealand (a division of Pearson New Zealand Ltd)
Penguin Group (USA) Inc., 375 Hudson Street, New York,
New York 10014, USA
Penguin Group (Canada), 10 Alcorn Avenue, Toronto, Ontario,
Canada M4V 3B2 (a division of Pearson Penguin Canada Inc.)
Penguin Books Ltd, 80 Strand, London, WC2R 0RL, England
Penguin Ireland, 25 St Stephen's Green, Dublin 2, Ireland
(a division of Penguin Books Ltd)
Penguin Group (Australia), 250 Camberwell Road, Camberwell,
Victoria 3124, Australia (a division of Pearson Australia Group Pty Ltd)
Penguin Books India Pvt Ltd, 11, Community Centre, Panchsheel Park,
New Delhi - 110 017, India
Penguin Books (South Africa) (Pty) Ltd, 24 Sturdee Avenue, Rosebank,
Johannesburg 2196, South Africa

Penguin Books Ltd, Registered Offices: 80 Strand, London, WC2R 0RL, England

First published by Penguin Group (NZ), 2005
1 3 5 7 9 10 8 6 4 2

Copyright © Debbie Mayo-Smith 2005

The right of Debbie Mayo-Smith to be identified as the author of this work in
terms of section 96 of the Copyright Act 1994 is hereby asserted.

Designed by Shaun Jury
Typeset by Egan-Reid Ltd
Printed in Australia by McPherson's Printing Group

ISBN 0 14 302031 5
A catalogue record for this book is available
from the National Library of New Zealand.

www.penguin.co.nz

Contents

Preface

What this book is not

A computer manual on how to operate Outlook or Outlook Express. There are many manuals on the market fitting that requirement.

What this book is

A wonderful, strategic, easy reading 'how-to' for busy people already using Outlook, Outlook Express or any other email program.

My goal is to look at the most common problems you have with using email, your Calendar, Address Books/Contacts; and show you clever, timesaving solutions in a 'how-to' way.

What's more, if you're in business you'll love the added strategies to improve your marketing and email prowess. The time-saving tips will claw back absolutely hours wasted in your inbox. You'll pump up your personal productivity. **In fact this is a book that everyone who uses email should have!**

Enjoy!
Debbie Mayo-Smith

Terms used in this book

Title Bar | Button |

Menu/menu commands

Toolbar

Entire object window

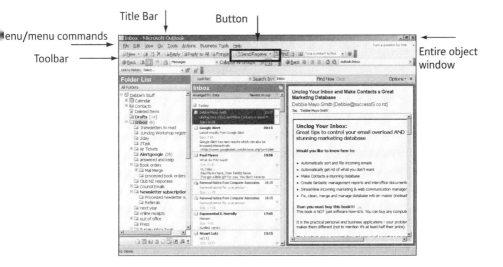

All the screen-shot illustrations in this book were taken from my personal Inbox using Microsoft® Outlook 2003 and Outlook Express 6.

Terms

Title bar

The bar containing the name of the window or document you are working with. It's the blue horizontal strip with the name of the document or folder written on it. The title bar of the item you're working on will be blue. The other windows open on your computer screen will be grey.

Menu bar

The bar below the title bar. It contains the names of menus (such as **File**, **Edit**, **View**, and **Insert**).

Menu commands
A list of instructions or actions to take (such as **Save, Print,** and **Open**) that open in a drop-down box when you select a menu bar item.

Toolbar
A bar (usually below the menu bar) with icons/buttons and options you use to carry out commands. They are normally grouped by category, such as **Standard, Formatting, Drawing**.

Button
A graphic element (icon) that performs a specific function. Buttons are similar to menu commands but they are graphical shortcuts. Several buttons make up a toolbar.

Window
What you have active on the screen. If you have several emails open, or both your Inbox and Contacts in different windows, your active window is the one with the blue title bar across the top.

Top Tip
More on Toolbars.

Different Microsoft® Office programs offer different toolbars. You probably don't want to see all of the available toolbars all the time.

To choose which toolbar(s) to view on your View menu, point to Toolbars and click the toolbar you want displayed.

Outlook Express *vs* Outlook

Outlook Express comes free with Internet Explorer. Outlook is purchased as part of the Microsoft® Office suite of programs. If all you want to do is send and receive emails, by all means just use Outlook Express. No problem.

But if you need more than just basic email send and receive, there's NO COMPETITION. Outlook wins. Hands down. Just check out the different features in Table 1 on the next page.

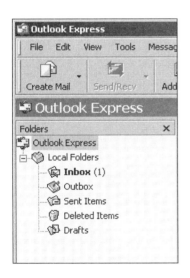 

Figure 1 *Outlook Express is very basic. In, Out, Sent, Deleted, and Drafts. The Address Book is simply that – just for basic contact details.*

Figure 2 *Outlook, on the other hand, has many more features. Calendar, Contacts (which you can do marvellous things with), Tasks (an automatic to-do list prompt), Journal, Junk Mail, Notes, and Archive.*
New in 2003 – Search Folders and Business Contact Manager, a new Contact Management tool that works with Outlook.

Table 1 *Comparing Outlook and Outlook Express*

PROGRAM FEATURES	OUTLOOK	OUTLOOK EXPRESS
Send and receive emails	Yes	Yes
Address Book and Contacts folder to store and retrieve email addresses	Yes	Yes
Multiple address books	Yes	No
Fully integrated Calendar, including meeting and event scheduling, appointments, and group calendars	Yes	No
Reminders for email messages, calendar events, tasks, and notes	Yes	No
Auto backup (archive). Store old items (that you want to keep but don't need immediate access to), and move those old items to the archive location automatically	Yes	No
Microsoft® Word as your email editor to provide access to additional formatting and style options	Yes	No
Categories for organising your items	Yes	No
Tasks folder to keep lists of personal or work-related errands that you want to track from start to finish	Yes	No
Junk email message filter	Yes	No
Notes folder (electronic equivalent of paper sticky notes)	Yes	No
Signatures and stationery	Yes	Yes
Secure email messaging	Yes	Yes

TAKE CONTROL OF YOUR INBOX

CHAPTER ONE

Help!
I have a huge quantity of
emails in my Inbox!

Solutions in this chapter

☑ Build your own Inbox filing cabinet with **Folders**

☑ Automate your email 'filing' with **Rules**

☑ Safely store old emails in **Archives**

Folders – your own Inbox filing cabinet

Folders are the backbone of your Inbox

Just as you organise your normal computer work into folders and subfolders, you should set them up in your Outlook/Outlook Express program too.

Why? Two great reasons

First, it's a stunning way to be neat and organised. Like putting your clothes away in the drawers they belong in, or colour coding your clothes in your closet. When you need a specific email, you know exactly where it is stored instead of hunting through possibly hundreds (or thousands) of emails lined up in your Inbox.

Once you have set up your folders, you can drag & drop your read emails into them.

More importantly though, folders are **invaluable** when you start setting up Rules. Rules automatically sort and put your emails into folders as they arrive – bypassing your inbox. (More on Rules on pages 23–29).

HOW DO I CREATE A FOLDER?

(See Figure 1 for the shortcut.)

1. On your **File** menu, point to **New**. Click **Folder**.

2. In the **Name** box, enter a name for your folder.

3. In the **Folder Contains** box, click the type of folder you want to create.

4. In the **Select where to place the folder** list, click where you'd like it to go (such as a new Inbox folder, or one nested inside an existing folder.

Figure 1 *The shortcut for creating a new folder is to right-click an existing folder such as Inbox. Select New Folder. Then follow the directions as detailed above.*

Top Tip
Drag & drop – if you don't know this shortcut, it's worth the price of this book alone!

Place your mouse on anything, left-click and hold. Then move your mouse, dragging that item, and 'drop' it where you want it moved! You drop by releasing the mouse button.

For example, an email can be dragged from your Inbox to a folder. A document can be dragged from one folder location to another while in Windows® Explorer. A sentence can be highlighted in a document, then dragged & dropped to another location in that document.

Clever ideas!
Nested/subfolders

You can nest folders within folders (I call these subfolders).

For example, if you have an Inbox folder for online newsletters you receive, you can have a subfolder for ones that you have read and want to keep. To create subfolders, simply right-click the folder you want them nested in. Select **New Folder** and follow the instructions on page 20, under How do I create a folder?

Ordering folders the way you want them

Folders are stored alphabetically by default. However, you might find that folders important to you – or ones you use all the time in your Inbox – are low in the totem pole of alphabetical spelling. Therefore you always have to scroll to get to them.

Circumvent this by putting a letter or number in front of the normal folder name to bring it up to the top. You can see in Figure 2 that by titling my folders '*1Newsletters To Read; 2day; 2Task*' I made them the first three folders in my Inbox. My *Air Tickets* folder has the subfolder *flown* inside it.

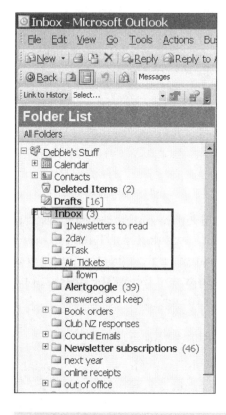

Figure 2 *Nested folders are indented below their parent folder. Letters or numbers before names place folders in the order you desire. 'flown' is my subfolder in 'Air Tickets'. I placed the number 1 before 'Newsletters to read' and brought that folder to the very top of the folder lineup in my Inbox.*

HOW DO I CHECK THE SIZE OF MY FOLDER?

1. Right-click the folder.

2. Select **Properties**.

3. Click on **Folder Size**.

HOW DO I GROUP EMAILS BY SIZE?

On the **View** menu, point to **Arrange By**, and click **Size**.

Rules
The magic of Rules

Your automatic eyes and hands.

Aah! If you don't know about Rules, this could be a life-changing experience for you – I sincerely mean it. Well, if you spend a lot of time in your Inbox it will be.

If you *do* know about Rules, I suggest you sit back and have a little think about how you can use them more frequently and creatively to manage your emails. Or go straight to Appendix IV on page 262 now and browse through some of my suggestions. These could save you hours a week!

Rules help you manage your emails by looking at them and then performing actions you specify that match conditions you set.

Rules can look at, for example:

- Emails from a certain email address.
- Emails not directly addressed to you.
- Certain words in the subject line or the body of the email.

Actions can be set for incoming or outgoing emails

For example, you could:

- Have emails from your mother go into your MUM folder.
- Send newsletters into a newsletter folder.
- Put etickets into your travel folder.
- Look for the word Viagra and have that email go straight to Deleted Items without it ever passing in front of your eyes.
- Have a copy of every email you send go into a specified folder.

Top Tip
One of the clever individuals in my Inbox workshop set a Rule to delay sending his emails. After he pushes the send button, a 10-minute lag occurs until it's actually sent. He calls this his 'rethinking' time in case there are ever changes that need to be made.

See how wonderful Rules can be?

Types of Rules

Rules fall into two general categories: **Notification** and **Organisation**.

Notification Rules

Alert you in some way when you receive a particular email. You can be hi-tech, and (for example) create a Rule that automatically sends a message to your mobile phone when you receive an email from a family member or an enquiry from your website asking for a quote.

Organisation Rules

Perform one or more actions on an email. For example, Head Office emails could go into a Head Office folder. Orders from your website can go to a folder (so you know an order came in), then a Rule can automatically copy and forward them to an assistant for handling. You can create a Rule that flags an email for follow-up on a particular day.

The more Rules you have, the more you automate your filing of emails. Thinking laterally, it also forms a hierarchy of incoming email importance for you.

HOW WILL I KNOW IF I'VE GOT NEW MAIL?

You might be thinking, 'Great, Debbie – , but how will I know a new email has arrived if I have it go straight to a folder?'

Have you noticed that when you have new emails in your Inbox, the word 'Inbox' becomes bold with a blue number next to it? The blue number indicates the number of new and unread emails.

It's the same for Rules. All the folders holding new and unread emails will be bold with a blue number next to them (See Figure 3.)

Figure 3 *You'll know when a Rule has placed a new message into a folder – the folder name turns bold and the number of new and unread emails appears to the right in blue.*

In this example you'll see that for my newsletter, I have changes of address and unsubscribes go directly to their proper folders – instead of cluttering my Inbox.

Top Tip

If you do newsletters, create a Rule looking for the words 'out of office' and permutations thereof. Let the Rule put these incoming emails into a folder or delete them. Turn it on when you send out the newsletter. Turn it off a short while after you've sent your newsletter. Ahhh, you don't have to deal with those bothersome 'out of office' messages in your Inbox anymore!

Top Tip

When you combine Folders, Rules and creative thinking, you'll see you can save yourself literally hours and hours a month.

Think about common incoming emails – what Rules can you create to sort them, and what folders do you need to hold them? Don't forget to turn to Appendix IV on page 262 for great Rule ideas.

Using Rules and the Rules Wizard

WHERE DO I GO TO CREATE A RULE?

1. There are several ways to create Rules:

- Select the **Rule icon** from your Toolbar (Outlook only).
- Or right-click the email (Outlook 2003 Only).
- In **Outlook** on the **Tools** menu, click **Rules and Alerts** (Figure 5).

- **In Outlook Express** on the **Tools** menu, click **Message Rules**, then select **Mail** (Figure 6).

2. Click **New Rule**. And go from there. The world is your oyster with all the options Rules Wizard gives you.

> **Top Tip**
>
> Hate those Cc's and Bcc's?
>
> Create folders/rules to keep them out of your Inbox and into their own Bcc and Cc Folder.

There is a wonderful Rules Wizard that walks you through how to set up your own rules. Here are a few rule options.

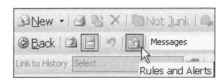

Figure 4 *The Rules icon on your toolbar looks like a folder opening and an email falling in.*

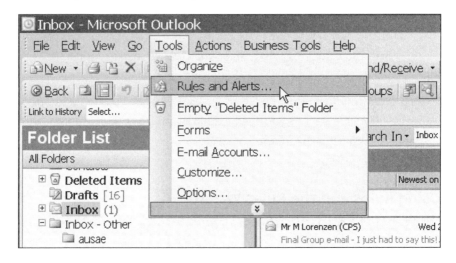

Figure 5 *Tools > Rules and Alerts in Outlook.*

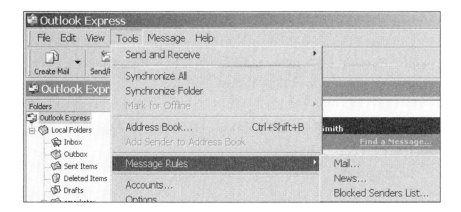

Figure 6 *Outlook Express Tools ˃ Message Rules.*

HOW DO I CREATE A RULE WITH MY OWN CONDITIONS, ACTIONS, AND EXCEPTIONS?

1. Click **Start from a blank rule,** and then click **Next.**

2. Under **Select when messages should be checked**, select **Check messages when they arrive** or **Check messages after sending,** and then click **Next.**

3. Follow the rest of the instructions in the **Rules Wizard.**

If you want to run this rule on emails already in one of your folders, select the **Run this rule now on emails already in** *'folder'* check box on the last step of the Rules Wizard.

To have this rule apply to *all* your email accounts and Inboxes, select the **Create this rule on all accounts** check box on the last step of the Rules Wizard.

HOW DO I CREATE A RULE BASED ON AN EMAIL IN A FOLDER?

1. Open the folder that contains the email.

2. Right-click the email you want to base your new Rule on.

3. Click **Create Rule.**

4. In the **Create Rule** dialogue box, select the conditions and

actions you want to apply.

5. To add more conditions, actions, or exceptions to the Rule, click **Advanced Options**, and then follow the rest of the instructions in the Rules Wizard.

HOW DO I CREATE A RULE BASED ON AN EMAIL I AM COMPOSING?

1. Add who you want to send the email to, or type a subject for the email.

2. Click the **Create Rule** icon on the toolbar.

3. In the **Create Rule** dialogue box, select the conditions and actions you want to apply.

4. To add more conditions, actions, or exceptions to the rule, click **Advanced Options**, and then follow the rest of the instructions in the Rules Wizard.

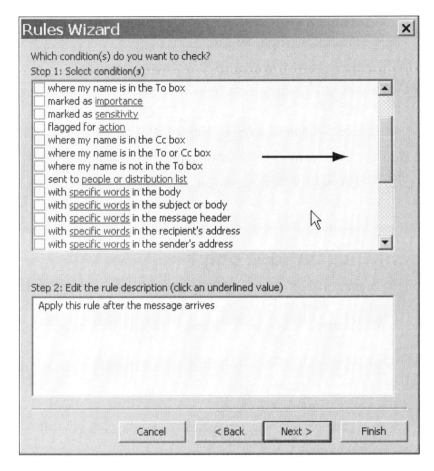

Figure 7 *You have wonderful flexibility when creating Rules with all the options available. Look at all those conditions – and there's still so much scroll remaining!*

HOW DO I CREATE A RULE BASED ON A NAME OR DISTRIBUTION LIST IN AN EMAIL?

1. Open the email you want to base your Rule on.

2. Right-click the name or distribution list in the **From, To,** or **Cc** list, and then click **Create Rule**.

3. In the **Create Rule** dialogue box, select the conditions and actions you want to apply.

4. To add more conditions, actions, or exceptions to the Rule,

click **Advanced Options,** and then follow the rest of the instructions in the Rules Wizard.

Archiving (Outlook only)

Your Outlook mailbox grows as you create and receive items. It also becomes dated. Why carry around emails that are two years old? Or meetings/appointments in your calendar that are four months old? Or old eticket receipts?

Archiving is a brilliant answer. Why?

1. **Effective record keeping**

   By archiving instead of deleting emails, you'll keep records.

2. **Save disk space**

   Archiving uses compression, so archived items use less storage space.

3. **Your Outlook opens faster**

   Because it's lost weight. My cheeky way of saying you've shifted file-size out.

4. **Cuts down on your clutter**

   Archiving removes items from your mailbox and puts them in the archive file.

5. **It's automatic**

   Archiving works automatically. You'll get a little prompt saying 'Want to archive your old items now?' And all you have to do is click **Yes.**

> **Top Tip**
> Let's cover this now – what's an item?
>
> An **Item** is the basic element that holds information in Outlook.
> Items include emails, appointments, contacts, tasks, journal entries, notes,
> posted items and documents.

AutoArchive

AutoArchive is on by default and runs automatically at scheduled intervals, clearing out old and expired items from your folders (except Contacts). Old items are those that reach the archiving age you specify. It could be four months, it could be two months. It could be one year. The choice is yours.

Expiration dates are optional. You can define them at the time you create the item, or at a later date. When the item expires, its unavailable and has a strike-out mark through it.

What AutoArchive does with items

AutoArchive can do one or both of the following things for you:

1. Permanently delete expired items.

2. Delete or archive old items to an archive file.

The archive file is a special type of data file. The first time AutoArchive runs, Outlook creates the archive file automatically in the following location:

C:\Documents and Settings*yourusername* \Local Settings\
Application Data\Microsoft\Outlook\Archive.pst

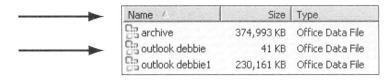

Name	Size	Type
archive	374,993 KB	Office Data File
outlook debbie	41 KB	Office Data File
outlook debbie1	230,161 KB	Office Data File

Figure 8 *Here are my Outlook files. 'outlook debbie1' is all my current Outlook information – contacts, calendar and emails. The older information is stored in a separate data file called 'archive' (but it is viewed in one's Inbox). Isn't it better to only carry around 230 megs of information instead of 605 megs? Result: Outlook is quicker to open.*

If you don't see the **Local Settings** folder, it may be hidden. See Microsoft® Windows Help for information about showing hidden folders.

Archives mirror your folder setup

When Outlook archives, it will set up a list of folders that exactly match what you have in Outlook. They're all nested under **Archive Folders** in your Outlook **Folder List**. Alternatively, you can have separate archive files for individual folders.

You work with the Archive emails the same way you work with items in your main Inbox. If you decide you want archived items moved back into your main mailbox, you can import all of them from the archive file into their original folders or into other folders you specify. Or you can manually move or copy individual items.

Top Tip
In one of my Inbox workshops, an attendee said he archived by year.

HOW DO I CHANGE HOW AUTOARCHIVE WORKS?

There are two types of AutoArchive settings. *Across the board* (global or default) and *per-folder* settings.

Company retention policies
By the way, archiving policies set by your company will override what you select, as they will take precedence.

HOW DO I VIEW ARCHIVED ITEMS?

1. If you're not in Folder view, on your **Go** menu, click **Folder List**.

2. Click on **Archive Folders** (or the name you specified for the archive location).

Top Tip

Not sure where your archive folder is?

To see where your archive folder is stored, right-click the Archive Folders folder in your Folder List. Click Properties for Archive Folders. Click Advanced, and then look at the File name box.

HOW DO I VIEW, CHANGE OR TURN OFF MY ARCHIVE SETTINGS?

1. On the **Tools** menu, click **Options.** Click the **Other** tab.

2. Select **AutoArchive**.

3. Review the menu, making the changes you want.

HOW DO I RUN AUTOARCHIVE AT ANY TIME?

1. On the **Tools** menu, click **Mailbox Cleanup**.

2. Click **AutoArchive**.

HOW DO I ARCHIVE A SINGLE FOLDER?

1. Select the folder that you want to archive.

2. On the **File** menu, click **Archive**.

Top Tip

Microsoft Online Tutorial – Manage the size of your mailbox:
http://office.microsoft.com/training/training.aspx?AssetID=
RC010294911033

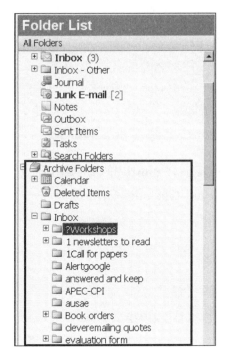

Figure 9 *Archives live in an identical folder structure in your Outlook (here's my Archive view). Now, for those smartypants checking out my other illustrations, remember Archives hold historical information. So if you add a new folder, it won't be in Archives until the right time period. Conversely, if you've deleted a folder in your Inbox it still can show in your Archives.*

8 More great tips

How do I . . .

1. SPEED UP EXPORTING AND ARCHIVING ITEMS?

Make exports and archives of your Outlook mailbox faster by emptying the **Deleted Items** folder first. Right-click the **Deleted Items** folder, and then click **Empty 'Deleted Items' Folder**.

2. DO A QUICK MAILBOX CLEAN-UP?

a. On the **Tools** menu, click **Mailbox Cleanup**.

b. Select options to find items that are old or large, and then move or delete them.

c. Click **AutoArchive** to move old items to **Archive Folders**, or click **Empty** to permanently delete items from your **Deleted Items** folder.

3. VIEW ALL MY UNREAD EMAILS IN MY INBOX?

On the **View** menu, point to **Arrange By**, point to **Current View**, and then click **Unread Messages in This Folder**.

4. QUICKLY PRINT?

Right-click the item, and then click **Print** on the shortcut menu.

5. QUICKLY ATTACH A FILE?

Open the item, and then on the **Insert** menu, click **File**. Locate the file you want to attach.

6. SEE WHERE OUTLOOK STORES MY MAIL, CALENDAR, AND CONTACTS DATA? (USEFUL TO KNOW FOR BACKING UP.)

a. On the **Tools** menu, click **Options**.

b. Click the **Mail Setup** tab, and then click **Data files**.

c. Folder locations are listed in the **Outlook Data files** dialogue box.

d. Select a data file, and then click **Open Folder**.

7. ALWAYS CHECK MY SPELLING?

On the **Tools** menu, click **Options**. Click **Preferences**, and then on the **Spelling** tab, select options to allow Outlook to correct your spelling. This can include creating a custom dictionary of frequently used terms, and choosing a dictionary in another language to check your spelling.

8. EMPTY MY DELETED ITEMS WHEN I CLOSE OUTLOOK?

- **Automatically:**
  On the **Tools** menu, click **Options**, and click the **Other** tab. Under **General**, select the **Empty the Deleted Items** folder upon exiting check box.

- **Manually**:
  Right-click the **Deleted Items** folder and click **Empty 'Deleted Items' Folder** on the shortcut menu, or click **Empty 'Deleted Items' Folder** on the **Tools** menu.

CHAPTER TWO

Help! Do I really have to open these emails to read them?

Solutions in this chapter

☑ Read emails without opening them, in **Preview**

☑ Set up **Rules** to read emails for you first

Don't open that email!

Often you can't gauge an email's content or importance by just seeing who it's from and reading the subject line.

Big time-waster

You might not have thought of it before, but count the seconds that elapse from when you double-click an email (to read it) to when it opens on your screen. To calculate how much time you waste, multiply it by the number of emails you get in a day (a week, 12 months). You'd be astonished by the needless time wasted.

You can immediately grab this time back. In fact, theoretically you will never have to open an email again (well, almost).

Previewing Emails

Three options of looking at an email without opening it

1. **AutoPreview** – you'll see the first three lines of each new unread email (Figure 1). However, for colourful emails (HTML) you'll often just see the HTML coding of images and normally invisible instructions (Figure 2).

2. **Preview** – you'll see the email in its entirety. You can scroll through the email and read it without ever opening it. You might be familiar with Preview in the bottom half of your screen. With the new Outlook 2003, you can now preview vertically. Outlook 2003 has also changed the name to **Reading Pane** (Figure 3).

3. **Both the AutoPreview and the Preview/Reading Pane are turned on**.

> **Top Tip**
> What is HTML?
>
> The letters stand for HyperText Markup Language. Very simply, computers can only 'see' text, they can't 'see' formatting. Think, 'typewriter'. HTML is a code that tells the computer to format the text and where to get images from; for example, using the font Arial and making the text bold and large. Add colour here, stick a picture exactly over there, put this in italics, place this in a table . . . Catch my drift? The HTML code transforms what we would see as plain typewriting to a page or email with colour, formatting and images.

Previewing emails in Outlook

By the way, this works for your **Contacts, Calendar** and **Task** items too!

1. AutoPreview (the first three lines) all emails
On the **View** menu, click **AutoPreview**.

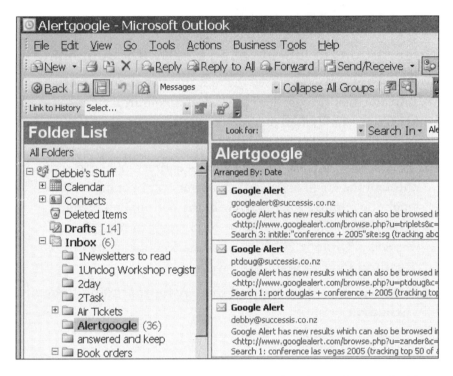

Figure 1 *AutoPreview allows you to see the first three lines of an email without opening it.*

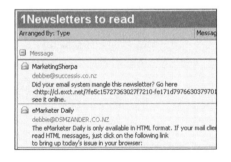

Figure 2 *When you receive colourful (HTML) emails, often the AutoPreview just shows HTML coding or hidden messages.*

If you only want your unread emails to Auto Preview

a. On the **View** menu, point to **Arrange By**, point to **Current View**, and then click **Customize Current View**.

b. Click **Other Settings**, and then click **Preview unread items**.

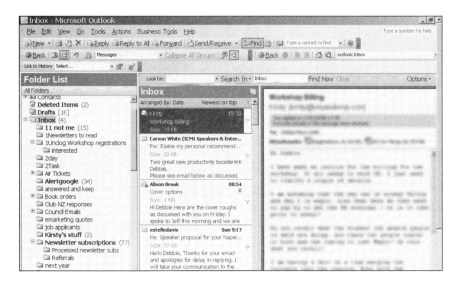

Figure 3 *The Preview/Reading Pane shows the email in a window. You might be familiar with seeing this window under your emails. Outlook 2003 offers an additional choice – a vertical instead of a horizontal window – and renames it as Reading Pane. Note: Illustration is blurred for privacy reasons.*

2. Preview the entire content of your emails (In other words, read your emails without opening them.)

a. On the **View** menu, point to **Preview Pane** (2000–02) or **Reading Pane** (2003).

b. Click **Right** or **Bottom** (2003 only).

In the **Preview Pane/Reading Pane** you can read the content, open attachments, follow a hyperlink, use voting buttons (in Calendar), view the follow-up information in it, and respond to Meeting Requests.

By the way:

1. The Reading Pane is not available for the **Drafts** folder.

2. When you are viewing an email in the Reading Pane, you can view email properties about a name in the **From, To**, or **Cc** field by double-clicking it.

Previewing emails in Outlook Express

1. On the **View** menu, select **Layout**

   • You can select/deselect seeing the **Preview pane**.

   • You can see the **Reading Pane** below or to the right (Outlook Express 6).

HOW DO I CHANGE THE LOCATION OF MY READING PANE IN OUTLOOK 2003?

1. On the **View** menu, point to **Reading Pane**, and then click **Right** or **Bottom**.

2. To turn off the Reading Pane and view more of the list of emails, on the **View** menu, point to **Reading Pane**, and click **Off**.

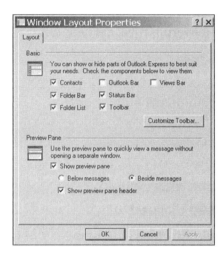

Figure 4 *With Outlook Express you can preview your emails by selecting Layout on the View menu.*

Top Tip
Resize the Preview/Reading Pane.

Point to the left border of the Reading Pane, and when the pointer becomes a double-headed arrow, drag the border to the left or right.

Rules

As we explained in Chapter One, Rules are a great way to automate your Inbox.

And what could be better than setting Rules up to 'read' your emails as they arrive, then send them to their proper folders? Get rid of the ones you don't want? In essence, do as much work for you as possible beforehand.

Appendix IV (page 262) has a long list of Rule suggestions to help you think of your own.

Get organised!

The more rules you put in place, the more organised you'll be in:

1. Giving the correct emails your priority attention.
2. Saving personal emails (at work) for a less busy time.
3. Filtering out emails from people covering their derrière (all those Cc's).
4. Getting rid of junk mail/spam.
5. Getting priority action on important items such as orders, customer service, and quotes.

Clever ideas!

Two more ideas to help you work more effectively.

Change when emails are marked as read

Whenever you read an email, the little envelope icon to the left of it goes from bold and closed, to open. When you look at an email in preview, after a certain amount of time it will mark itself 'read'.

But what if you don't want that to happen on a specific email? What if you want to quickly look at all your new emails and go back to specific ones later?

HOW DO I FIND A SPECIFIC EMAIL LATER, AND QUICKLY?

1. An option is to change it back to **Unread**. How?
   Simply right-click the email and select **Mark as Unread.**
2. Additionally, you can adjust the time lapse (how many seconds elapse before the email is marked 'read') to suit your needs.

Top Tip
Quickly mark an email as read.
Right-click the email and then click **Mark as Read**.

In Outlook:

a. On the **Tools** menu, select **Options,** and then select the **Other** tab.

b. Select **Preview/Reading Pane**.

c. Select the time and options you want.

In Outlook Express:

a. On the **Tools** menu, select **Options,** and then select the **Other** tab.

b. Select **Read Tab**.

c. Select the options you want.

Top Tip
If you would like to change marked as read to unread for one email or the contents of an entire folder, right-click your mouse (while on that email or in the folder) and select **Mark as unread**.

Hide the email header

If you want to maximise your ability to read the content of an email, and don't need to see who it's from and the subject line – you can hide the email header.

1. On the **View** menu, point to **Arrange By,** and then select **Custom**.

2. Click **Other Settings**.

3. Under **Preview/Reading Pane**, select the **Hide header information** check box. Note – you'll still see the header information in the AutoPreview in your Inbox. It just won't show in the preview.

4. To show email headers again, clear the **Hide header information** check box.

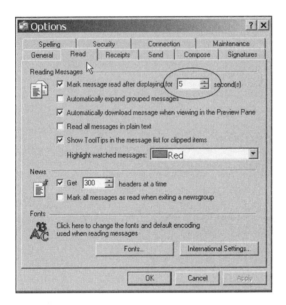

Figure 5 *To change the time lag to when your emails are marked as read in Outlook Express, you select Tools > Options > Read and make the changes you desire.*

Top Tip
Quickly read your emails without opening them.

To see the first three lines of each email, on the **View** menu, click **AutoPreview**.

To see the complete email to the right of the email list, on the **View** menu, point to **Preview/Reading Pane**.

CHAPTER THREE

Help!
I've lost an email!

Solutions in this chapter

- ☑ Common disappearing acts
- ☑ **Sorting** your emails
- ☑ How to **Find** that needle in the haystack
- ☑ New **Search Folders**

Where is it?!

Argh! We've all felt the aggravation of the missing email (plus file, entire folder of work, etc.) and the frustration of hunting for an email you know you have – but can't recall where you've put it. Or you can only remember a bit of the content and are having trouble finding it.

Don't despair – there are ways of finding emails, and also some common ways of making vanished ones reappear like a rabbit out of a hat.

Common disappearing acts

If you're looking for an email or a folder that has totally vanished into thin air, one of two things may have happened.

Accidental delete

First, you could have accidentally deleted it. This isn't a reason to panic (at least, not yet). Deleted items add up in your **Deleted Items** folder. They only hit the road forever when you personally empty the contents of that folder. And before the actual action of deleting happens, you'll be prompted to confirm if you're sure you want to permanently delete things.

So, go to your deleted items and look there for what you lost.

- Emails and email folders will be in the Outlook/Outlook Express Deleted Items folder.

- Documents and document folders will be in the Recycle bin (you can find it in Windows Explorer). It has a waste basket icon.

Dropped it somewhere

Second, and again a very common error, is that you may have accidentally dragged & dropped it somewhere without knowing. Chapter Six opens with the wonders and glories of drag & drop – but it does have this downside too. When you accidentally select something with your mouse, move the mouse and release it – bye bye to whatever it was holding. It's now relocated to where it landed.

Your solution is not to panic (oh, the number of times I have flipped out over my missing files!), but rather to search for it. Patiently and systematically, 100 to 1, you'll find it. And that's what this chapter is all about. Read on.

You'll learn about Sorting, Find, Advanced Find and Search folders, as well as colour coding emails and arranging them by conversational threads.

How do I Sort?

Quickest and easiest way

First on the list of simple ways to help you find your emails (and Contacts, Tasks, Sent items . . .) is **Sorting**.

You sort with a simple click on the top of the column header in your email list (To, From, Size, Date . . .). On your first click, it will sort alphabetically or chronologically by that field. Click it a second time, and it sorts alphabetically in descending order or from oldest to newest.

As an aside, it's now a good time to introduce the fact (if you didn't know it already) that you can view your Outlook information in many different ways.

We're most familiar with the 'table' view, where everything is in columns and rows. Chapter Twenty-one talks about different views, and gives examples. But take a moment to investigate if you haven't done so before.

Have a play and investigate other Viewing options

1. On the **View** menu click **Arrange By**.

2. Select **Current View**.

3. Select the arrangement you want. You might like the 'Last Seven Days'.

Additionally, you can add more fields (columns of information such as From, Size, Flags, Date) to View when you're looking at your emails and contacts, etc.). Turn to page 209 for instructions on how to do this (it works the same way as choosing fields in Contacts).

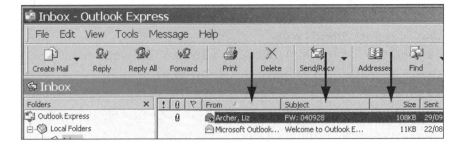

Figure 1 *Click the grey column header, and the contents of that folder will automatically sort by that field. Click it again, and it will sort the opposite way round.*

HOW DO I DO A CUSTOM SORT?

1. On the **View** menu, point to **Arrange By** and then click **Custom**.

2. Click **Sort**.

3. In the **Sort items by** box, click a **field** to sort by. If the field you want isn't in that box click a different field set in the **Select available fields from** box.

4. If the field you sort by is the same as the field that items are **grouped by**, Outlook sorts the group headings instead of the items within each group. To sort the individual items in a group, click a field in the **Sort items by** box that is different from the **Group by** field you have chosen.
   Note:
   A group is a set of items with one common attribute. Adding an item to a group is to combine items with a common attribute (such as: email received by the same person, on the same date or having the same subject) under a shared heading in a table.

5. Click **Ascending** or **Descending** for the sort order.

6. To sort by an additional field, click a field in the **Then by** box.

Top Tip
Microsoft Online Tutorial on colouring: http://office.microsoft.com/training/Training.aspx?AssetID=RC011156011033&CTT=6&Origin=RC0 11156011033

How do I find lost emails?

We'll start with several ways to search for that specific email (or Contact, or meeting, etc.), looking simply for words or email addresses, or names. Then we'll move on to more advanced filtering with Advanced Find to hone your search very specifically.

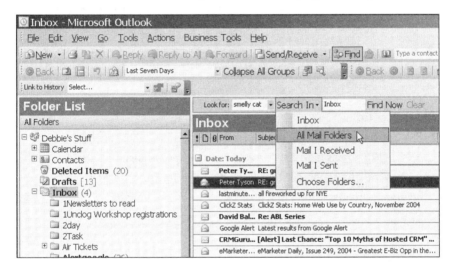

Figure 2 *To do a search you select Find, type in what words (email address, names, etc.) you are looking for, then select which folders you want Outlook to search. For this example I was going to look for the words smelly cat in any email in all my folders.*

OUTLOOK: HOW DO I SEARCH FOR AN ITEM CONTAINING A SPECIFIC WORD OR PHRASE?

1. Click **Find** on the **Standard** toolbar to display the **Find Bar**.

2. In the **Look for** box, type any text you want to search for in the most common fields of the item, or click the arrow on the **Look for** box to use previous search text.

3. Specify the folders you want to search.

Current folder

If you want to search within the current folder you're in (not its subfolders),

- Click **Find Now**.

Specific folder

If you want to search within a specific folder:

1. Click **Search In** then, click **Choose Folders**.

2. Select the folders you want to search (you can select more than one). To include subfolders, select the **Search subfolders** check box.

3. In Outlook 2003 you can save your search as a **Search Folder** – see page 54.

Top Tip

You can save the contents of a folder to a file, whether there is one or 100 emails in it! The file will be a text file; while email attachments *aren't* saved, the entire content (including the To, From, Date) is saved. The emails are just strung one after another in one long file.

To save one or more emails, highlight them, then select the **File** menu, and click **Save As**.

OUTLOOK EXPRESS: HOW DO I SEARCH FOR AN ITEM CONTAINING A SPECIFIC WORD OR PHRASE?

1. On the **Edit** menu, point to **Find**, and then click **Message**.

2. Enter criteria in the search fields.

Advanced Find

Advanced Find allows you to be very specific. You can filter your search using several factors, or search by options not available in the regular Find.

HOW DO I SEARCH FOR ITEMS OR FILES USING OTHER OR MULTIPLE CRITERIA?

1. On the **Tools** menu, point to **Find**.

2. Click **Advanced Find**.

3. In the **Look for** box, click the type of item or file you want to search for.

4. If the folder you want to search does not appear in the **Inbox**, or you want to search more than one folder, click **Browse** to select from a list.

5. Select the remaining search options you want. Note there are three different tabs (**Messages**, **More Choices** and **Advanced**).

6. Click **Find Now**.

How do I limit the search to a certain date?

1. Select the **Folders created since** check box, and then enter a date.

2. Click **Find Now**.

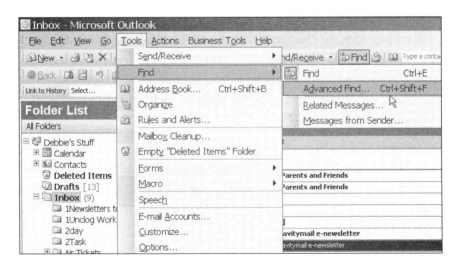

Figure 3 *Outlook's Advanced Find can be found either under Options in the Find toolbar or under Tools > Find > Advanced Find.*

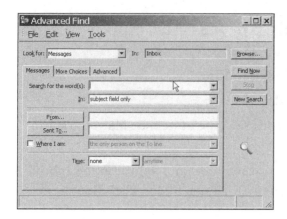

Figure 4 *Advanced Find offers many ways to fine-tune what you're looking for or to search for criteria other than that allowed in the normal Find.*

Search Folders (Outlook 2003)

Think of a Search Folder as a virtual folder. Once you have set your criteria, it will gather information on all the matching emails from all your different folders (including deleted and sent items). Your emails are not physically moved into these search folders. They reside where you have placed them. The Search folder is simply a permanent and growing record of emails that meet the criteria you set.

You might not think Search Folders are particularly exciting, but think how useful it is to be able to see different groupings of your emails without changing their folder location (your organisation of them) in any way. For example, if you wanted to see all the emails from the sports committee you're on, or emails from a co-worker in one place, or emails on a specific project – without moving them – you could use a Search Folder to do this.

Once you create a Search Folder, you can find it in the Navigation Pane or in your folder list. It's called **Search Folders** (duh!), and contains all the groups of search results you've created, as well as three default Search Folders: **For Follow Up**, **Large Mail**, and **Unread Mail**.

You can also carry out a search, and save the results as a Search Folder.

Note:

Search Folders for your Mailbox work only in your Mailbox; Search Folders for Archive Folders work only in Archive Folders.

When you view emails in a Search Folder, you can move them by drag & drop, or copy them to a normal folder, or delete them. And, of course, you can read them (or simply mark them as read).

However, you can't drag emails *into* a Search Folder; the only way an email can appear in a Search Folder is if it meets the criteria that you set up for the folder.

Figure 5 *Search Folders live below Tasks.*

Top Tip
Microsoft Tutorial on Search Folders:
http://office.microsoft.com/training/Training.aspx?AssetID=RC010778621033&CTT=6&Origin=RC010778621033

HOW DO I CREATE A SEARCH FOLDER?

1. On the **File** menu, point to **New**, and then click **Search Folder**.
2. Select one of the pre-defined **Search Folders,** or select the **Create a custom Search Folder** option, and fill in the criteria as appropriate.

HOW DO I SAVE MY CURRENT SEARCH AS A SEARCH FOLDER?

1. On the **Find Bar,** click **Options**.
2. Click **Save Search as Search Folder**.
3. Type a name for the Search Folder.

HOW DO I DELETE A SEARCH FOLDER?

1. In the Navigation Pane, right-click the **Search Folder**.
2. Click **Delete** *Search Folder* (where *Search Folder* is the specific name of the folder that you want to delete).

HOW DO I CUSTOMISE A SEARCH FOLDER?

Right-click the **Search Folder** that you want to customise, and click **Customize this Search Folder**.

Clever ideas!
Automatically colour code some of your emails

Do you scan your Inbox looking for emails from specific people or specific subjects? Would you like to quickly see which emails are of lower importance (such as you being Cc'd or Bcc'd in on the email)? Would you like emails from your loved ones to stand out? Then colour coding is right up your alley!

HOW DO I COLOUR CODE EMAILS FROM A SPECIFIC PERSON?

In the **Inbox**, select an email from someone important, such as your hubby, wife, boss or your mum.

1. On the Tools menu, click **Organize** to display the Organize pane.

2. In the left portion of the **Organize** pane, click **Using Colors**.

3. In the first bulleted item, you should see the word **from** and the name of the person who sent you the email.

4. Then you should see the word **in** and a drop-down list box. Click the arrow to select a colour (or you can keep the default colour).

5. Click **Apply Color**.

6. All of the emails in your Inbox from this person should now be colour coded with the colour you selected.

7. Take a look at the other colour options available in the **Organize** pane. Do you see how you could easily distinguish the emails that were sent only to you?

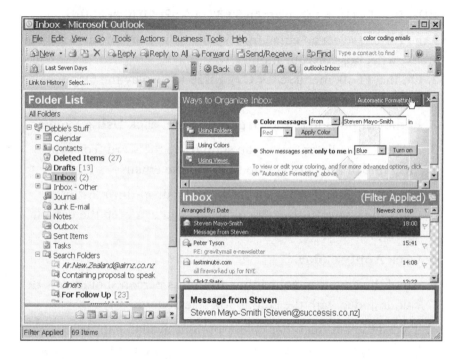

Figure 6 *By assigning red to the emails coming from Steven Mayo-Smith, I'll know immediately when my husband sends me an email. Turn on colour coding by selecting Tools > Organize > Using Colours.*

HOW DO I TURN OFF COLOUR CODING?

1. In the upper-right corner of the **Organize** pane, click **Automatic Formatting** (see Figure 6). **Note:** this button is available only when **Using Colors** is selected in the left portion of the **Organize** pane.

2. In the **Automatic Formatting** dialogue box, in the list of rules, select the one that says **Mail received from *important person*** (where important person is the name of the person who sent you the email you selected).

3. Clear the check box for the rule and click **OK**. Your emails should return to their original state (that is, not colour coded).

HOW DO I CHANGE THE COLOUR USED FOR AUTOMATIC FORMATTING?

1. Open the **Automatic Formatting** dialogue box.

2. In the **Automatic Formatting** dialogue box, scroll through the list of rules to find the one that says **Mail received from** *important person* – the person whose colour you want to change.

3. Click the rule to select it, and view the properties in the **Properties of selected rule** section of the dialogue box.

4. Click the **Font** button.

5. In the **Font** dialogue box, select a different colour than the one that is selected, and click **OK**.

6. Verify that the check box for the rule is selected, and click **OK**. The emails for your special person should now all be colour coded with the colour you selected.

HOW DO I DELETE A COLOUR CODING RULE?

1. Open the **Automatic Formatting** dialogue box.

2. Select the rule that you created.

3. Click the **Delete** button, and click **OK** to close the dialogue box.

Arrange emails by conversation

When emails are arranged by conversation, you can see the 'traffic flow' of a conversation. Emails are indented to show you who replied to whom. The dates show you when they replied. It could be committee members emailing back and forth and copying everyone in on it; it could be several employees having a say on a project. The common thread must be subject line of the email. This is what conversations are tracked on. (It ignores 're:' in case you're wondering.)

Top Tip

If you'd like to know more about sorting emails and reading by conversation thread, here's an online tutorial:

http://office.microsoft.com/training/Training.aspx?AssetID=RP0111561910 33&CTT=6&Origin=RC011156011033

5 More great sorting and searching tips
How do I . . .

1. SAVE SEARCHES THAT I USE OFTEN?

a. On the **Tools** menu, point to **Find** and then click **Advanced Find**.

b. In the **Advanced Find** dialogue box, specify your search criteria and click **Save Search** on the File menu.

c. You can share the search results with others by sending the search results file as an attachment in an email.

2. SEARCH FOR AND MOVE ITEMS OR FILES TO DIFFERENT FOLDERS?

a. On the **Tools** menu, point to **Find** and then click **Advanced Find**.

b. In the **Advanced Find** dialogue box, specify your search criteria and click **Find Now**.

c. After the results are displayed in the Search results window, move items to the folder of your choice.

3. SORT EMAILS ALPHABETICALLY BY SENDER NAME?

a. To sort, click **Arranged By** and then click **From**. To reverse the alphabetical order, click **From** again.

b. To sort by **Subject** line, click **Subject**. You can sort this way in any table in Outlook.

4. QUICKLY PRINT SEARCH RESULTS FROM MY INBOX?

To print a list of your search results from the **Advanced Find** dialogue box, press CTRL+P.

5. CREATE A SEARCH FOLDER QUICKLY FROM THE FIND BAR?

a. Press CTRL+E to open the **Find** bar.

b. Type what you want to find in the **Look for** box, specify which folder to look in by using the **Search In** box, and then click **Find Now**.

c. When the search is complete, click **Options** on the **Find** bar, and then click **Save Search as Search Folder**.

CHAPTER FOUR

Help! How do I stop receiving all this junk mail, or spam?

Solutions in this chapter

☑ Definition of junk mail, or spam

☑ **Junk** – how it finds you

☑ Being careful

☑ Getting rid of it before it arrives – **Filters**

☑ **Rule** your Inbox

Can the Spam Man!

No-one minds getting email. In fact, in study after study it's the most favoured form of communication.

At home, who wouldn't want an email from a friend or relative? For business communications – how much money has this little 'vehicle' saved when it acts as a carrier pigeon for those documents, records and reports? Remember those brown reusable inter-office envelopes that tied with a string and had name after name crossed off as they were used over and over to carry documents from one person to another? Or was that before your time?

What bothers us is getting irrelevant, untargeted, useless emails. Junk! And it's not just spam that could be considered junk. An email from a friend is useless if it's only a joke sent to many and you're not into that kind of thing. A business newsletter would be interesting reading to one individual, while it's useless junk to another.

So, how can you find the middle ground in this love/hate relationship with email? By being smart, taking precautions, and filtering. That's the key to win the war on junk.

Top Tip

Junk. Spam. What's in a name?

Most people use these two interchangeably. It's unwanted and unasked-for email. Most often, we think of spam as the overseas adult content or 'where on earth did they find me' emails. We consider junk as email from companies we might know, but just didn't want.

The story goes that when unsolicited email marketing (commonly called spam) arrived on the Internet, users were reminded of a popular Monty Python television show skit: a waiter, questioned by a customer, would reply to each question 'it comes with spam'. ('Well, we have spam; tomato & spam, egg & spam, egg, bacon & spam'.) Spam is a trademarked Hormel meat product that was well known in the US Armed Forces during World War II.

How does spam/junk mail find me?

Three ways:

1. Spider software

2. List purchase

3. Guessing email addresses.

1. Spider software

There are software programs that use web-crawling robots (called spiders) to swiftly go through websites gathering email addresses.

The spider will be given key words – such as financial, health, home, etc. It will look for web pages with these words and then seek and grab any email addresses it sees, building enormous lists.

2. List Purchase

Lists are compiled mainly in two ways.

1. When you join a mailing list, one of the normal small-print details is allowing your email address to be shared with others for relevant email communications.

2. The other way is when people manually go through public lists looking for email addresses – such as taking them from sections of the printed Yellow Pages®, company directories and listings, company and association websites. They figure since you have a published email address, you're agreeing to receive material that is relevant to you. Hah! That's the killer – who decides what is relevant for you?

3. Guessing email addresses

Spammers will automatically generate email addresses by guessing, based on domain names. For example, they'll start with xtra.co.nz or bigpond.com, and then just start adding hundreds of thousands of variations in front of the domain. Then out go millions of spam emails without testing the validity of email addresses. When an individual receives one of these emails and opens it, it sends a signal back to the spammer saying 'hey, you've got a live one here'.

In other words it verifies it's an *actual* email address. And then the flood begins.

If you'd like to know technically what happens, they actually put a one-pixel graphic link into the colourful **HTML** email. **HTML** is simply coding, it cannot 'carry' graphics (in other words, it cannot embed graphics in the emails). Instead, they carry a link to the graphic that is on a webserver. When you open the email, your computer sends a signal to that webserver saying 'download' – show me the picture, please. Because of its minute size, it is invisible to you.

By the way, only Outlook/Outlook Express 2000 and onwards can 'carry' graphics in the emails, but these are not true HTML emails.

This is one of the reasons for the new innovation in the Outlook 2003 Junk Mail Filtering system. Outlook 2003 automatically bans the automatic downloading of any graphics from webservers (see Figure 1). It does it because of this very reason (and also because the links have been known to lead viruses into your computer). Instead of seeing graphics, you'll see 'Right-click here to download pictures. To help protect your privacy, Outlook prevented automatic download of this picture from the Internet'.

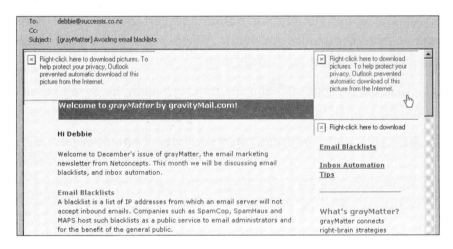

Figure 1 *How Outlook 2003 will display an email you receive that has graphics.*

As explained in Chapter 12, this is terrible news for genuine companies using email with clients, but it should help eliminate unwanted emails over time.

By the way, if you respond by answering back to spam sent to you in a *plain text* email – you also verify you're a live email address.

So how do I reduce the amount of junk mail/spam that I deal with?

Four ways:

1. Taking precautions

2. Corporate or ISP filtering

3. Using Outlook/Outlook Express junk mail filters

4. Creating your own rules.

1. Take precautions

a. Avoid replying to the sender

When you reply to unsolicited (unasked-for) emails and request to be removed from their list, it's another way of letting the spammers know that they've hit not only a live email address but one with a person that reads unsolicited email! Do note we are talking about spam, not about the regular online newsletters and emails you receive from companies you know. When you want to leave these mailing lists, it's absolutely okay to ask to unsubscribe.

The best way to 'opt out' of a spammer's mailing list is to pretend you never received the email.

b. Alter your email address when you have it online or post it

You might post your email address sometimes to a newsgroup, chat room, or bulletin board. Or of course put it on your website, the company website or an association website.

But you don't have to put it correctly. You can 'munge' your address. This means adding a character, number, or symbol that has to be taken out for your address to work – for example, debbie@su(ccessis.co.nz. You just tell people reading the address online in the text to fix it. This way, the automatic web crawlers harvesting your email address will never get a email delivered to you.

c. Be precious with your main email address

Create a 'throw away' Web email address (such as a Hotmail or

Yahoo one), and use that when registering for free software or shareware, or even when ordering from a company online.

d. Review website privacy policies

Read those online forms. Be sure to check all the privacy options, even though sometimes they're hard to find or there are several boxes to check.

e. Don't list yourself in Internet directories

f. DO NOT forward chain email

2. Corporate and ISP email filtering

Chapter 12 covers Corporate and ISP email filtering in detail, starting on page 136. However that chapter is written from the perspective of how to get your emails through.

Briefly, many companies now purchase email filtering software that reviews every email that comes into the company (and goes out – and around). Based on the criteria set by the company and IT manager, it will vet what is allowed to be delivered. You can be certain that if you work for a medium or large company, they have a filter on and you're not even seeing a fraction of what is actually being delivered.

Ditto for ISPs (your Internet Service Provider). Most of them have a filter on. You have the option of having them delete it on the spot, or allowing it to accrue in your web mail (mail received but not delivered), where you can check it.

3. Use Outlook/Outlook Express junk mail filters

Let's review Outlook 2003, Outlook 2000, and Outlook Express in that order.

Outlook 2003 Junk Mail Filter

The new Junk Mail Filter replaces the rules used in previous versions of Microsoft® Outlook. When you install Outlook, the Junk Mail Filter is on by default, with the protection level set to **Low**. This is designed to catch the most obvious junk and put it into a **Junk E-mail folder** (where you can review it). You can crank up the filter to **High,** but it will mistakenly catch 'good' emails too.

There are two parts to the new Junk Mail Filter:
1. The Junk Mail Filter lists (see below).
2. The behind-the-scenes coding that evaluates whether an unread email should be treated as a junk email – the criteria being content, structure and the time it was sent (for example).

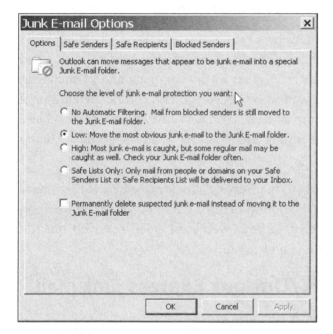

Figure 2 *The new Outlook 2003 Junk Mail Filter offers new built-in options: None, Low, High, and Safe Lists Only.*

Junk Mail Filter lists

You have five Junk Mail Filter lists with Outlook 2003.

Filters 4 and 5 block unwanted emails that come from another country or region, or appear in another language.

Big note here:
Graphics in emails will only be automatically downloaded (shown) in emails from those individuals or domains on your Safe Senders and Safe Recipients lists. However, you must physically add them. It isn't sufficient for them to be in your **Contacts**.

1. Safe Senders list:

This is a list of domain names and email addresses that you want to receive emails from.

Email addresses in **Contacts** are included in this list by default, so emails from people in your **Contacts** folder will never be treated as junk emails.

Emails from people in your **Contacts** will not be put in your junk mail. However, to have graphics that are in their emails automatically shown you must first physically add them to your **Safe Senders** list.

Email addresses of people who are not necessarily in your **Contacts** folder – but *are* people whom you correspond with regularly – are included in this list by default through the **Automatically add people I email to the Safe Senders list** check box.

Note:
- The recipient's email address is saved by default only when you create and send the email the usual way in Outlook, as opposed to a email generated automatically by a program.
- Distribution lists (Groups) will not be added by using this check box.

- If you are using a Microsoft® Exchange Server email account, names and email addresses in the **Global Address List** are automatically considered safe.

- You can also configure Outlook to accept emails only from people on your Safe Senders List, giving you total control over which emails are delivered to your **Inbox**. *I highly recommend that you don't, though, if you're in business. You will block emails from any new or potential client or any website enquiry!*

2. Safe Recipients list

A list of mailing lists or other subscription domain names and email addresses that you belong to and want to receive emails from. If you belong to mailing lists or distribution lists, you can add these names to your **Safe Recipients List** so that any emails sent to these email addresses or domain names will never be treated as junk, regardless of the content of the email.

3. Blocked Senders list

A list of domain names and email addresses that you want to be blocked. Email addresses and domain names on this list are always treated as junk email or spam.

4. Blocked Encodings list

A list that allows you to block a language encoding or character set in order to filter out unwanted international emails that display in a language you don't understand.

5. Blocked Top-Level Domains list

A list that allows you to block top-level country/region domains. This allows you to filter unwanted emails from specific countries or regions. For example, you could block all emails from China, Poland or Uganda.

1. **One at a time.**
   In the **Junk E-mail** folder, select a message and click **Delete** on the **Standard** toolbar.

2. **All at once.**
   Right-click the **Junk E-mail** folder in the **Navigation Pane**, and click **Empty Junk E-mail**.

3. **Permanently delete all the messages.**

a. Right-click the **Junk E-mail** folder in the **Navigation Pane**.

b. Press SHIFT while you click **Empty Junk E-mail Folder**.

Outlook 2000

Outlook 2000 doesn't hold a candle to the 2003 version. But then again, it's over five years old and junk mail didn't approximate what it does today. Outlook 2000 has a Junk and Adult Content filter as well as a Blocked Senders list.

The filtering occurs when you turn Junk Mail on. It's found under the **Organize** button.

1. Click the **Organize** button on the **Standard** toolbar in Outlook.

2. Click the **Turn on Junk E-mail** button. There's also an **Adult Content** button.

3. If you go into the **Using Colors** section, you can assign a colour to your Junk or Adult Content mail received. Simply click on the **colour drop-down boxes** so that they read **Color** and then select your choice of **colour** from the second drop-down box.

4. Additionally, you can set **Junk** or **Adult Content mail** to be moved to another folder or even be deleted, by altering the drop-down boxes so that they read **Move** and then selecting

Junk Mail, Deleted Items or another folder.

5. Once you have set up your chosen method of dealing with the mail, click on the **Turn on** button to activate it.

HOW DO I ADD A NEW SENDER TO THE BLOCKED SENDERS LIST?

If you receive an email from someone that you deem junk (or adult), you can add to Outlook's internal list of blocked senders.

1. In your **Inbox**, right-click on the email and select **Junk E-mail**.

2. Choose whether the sender belongs in the **Junk** or **Adult Content** list by clicking on either **Add to Junk Senders list** or **Add to Adult Content Senders list**.

3. An email will be displayed telling you where to view the list of blocked senders.

4. Click **OK**.

HOW DO I VIEW OR EDIT MY LIST OF BLOCKED SENDERS?

It is possible to view and edit your personal list of Junk or Adult Content senders.

1. In the **Standard** toolbar, click the **Organize** button.

2. Click either **Edit Junk Senders** or **Edit Adult Content Senders**.

3. Click on the **Add** button to add in new email addresses to the list.

4. Click on the **Edit** button to edit existing email addresses.

5. You can delete existing entries by selecting the email address in question and clicking on the **Delete** button.

Outlook Express

Now don't hold your breath. The only thing you can do is block senders – which in reality for spam is totally useless (I'm sure you've found this out for yourself already). Why? Spammers are wise to this ploy and use different email addresses. By the way, the emails you block go directly into your Deleted Items folder.

HOW DO I BLOCK EMAILS FROM AN INDIVIDUAL OR DOMAIN?

When you block a sender or domain, no email or news message from that sender or domain will arrive in your Inbox or in the news messages you read. Newsgroup messages from blocked senders are not displayed.

1. Highlight an email in your Inbox or the list of messages in a newsgroup from senders you want to block.

2. On the **Message** menu, click **Block Sender**.

Note: Blocking a sender does not apply to web (Hotmail) emails.

Done an oops?

Need to take someone you blocked by accident off the list?

To remove a name from the **Blocked Senders** list, click the **Tools** menu, point to **Message Rules**, and then click **Blocked Senders list**.

One last thing before Rules

You might not have noticed before reading this book, but one way spammers get around these filters is by sending their 'messages' in graphic form. So instead of writing the words Viagra and sex and stock picks, they'll have a graphic with the words as in Figure 4.

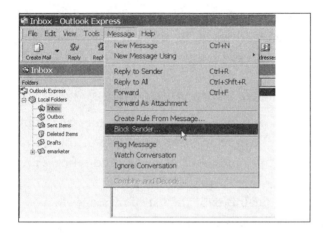

Figure 3 *Junk Mail blocking ability is limited in Outlook Express.*

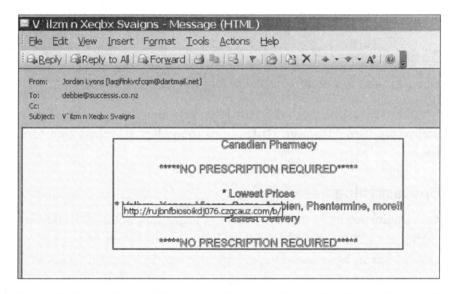

Figure 4 *Hmmm. The email is from Jordan Lyons. But look at his email address! And the content of the email. It's a singular graphic. You can read it, but all the filters see is the http address.*

4. Create personal Rules

If you didn't know about Rules before reading this book, you've just learnt all about them in Chapter One.

If you create Rules with junk mail in mind, you can significantly improve your management of junk mail in the future. You'll never be able to delete junk mail entirely. I notice from my Inbox that different blasts happen all the time. I might get a barrage of Create DVDs one day, while the next it's Do You Play Penny Stocks. The new function on Outlook 2003 – where you right-click an email and swiftly create a Rule based on that email – works stunningly in this instance.

HOW DO I EFFECTIVELY MANAGE WITH RULES?

You'll need to think about the junk mail you get. What annoys you? What is graphical? What email addresses is the junk coming in to?

I suggest picking out key words that are repeated, and variations thereof. Put all these words in a single Rule or several Rules. Have the Rule be dependent on seeing one of those words or phrases in the subject line or body of the email. You might even have only emails addressed to you in the **To** column go directly into your Inbox, while all others get put in another folder for you to review as a second priority.

Don't forget there is a long list of suggestions for Rules in Appendix IV.

Top Tip

Was an important email sent to the Junk Email folder?

If an item gets moved to your **Junk E-mail** folder by mistake, select the email, and then press CRTL+ALT+J.

Top Tip

Here's an idea for three simple rules:

1. All emails addressed to you stay in your Inbox.

2. All emails with you in the Cc or Bcc go to a Cc/Bcc folder.

3. All emails not addressed to you, or where your name is not in the Cc/Bcc, go into an All Others folder.

HOW DO I SEPARATE OUT EMAILS FROM PEOPLE NOT IN MY ADDRESS BOOK?

Create a filter moving all email NOT from people in your address book to a different folder.

Outlook 2002 and 2003 have rules conditions for 'sender is in specified address book'. Create a rule using this condition to move emails to a new folder, or use it as an exception to a rule which moves all other mail to another folder.

MAKE YOUR INBOX WORK FOR YOU

CHAPTER FIVE

Help!
I keep forgetting to follow
up on things!

Solutions in this chapter

☑ Automate your memory with **Outlook Tasks**

☑ Reminders and prompts with **Flags**

Automate your memory and throw those scraps of paper away

Have you ever received an email from a friend, waited a few days, and then forgotten to reply?

How about an email alerting you to a special event – but two days after the event you remembered it?

What if you got a proposal or a quote on work to be done on your home, and you wanted to follow up in a few days? Or conversely, you've sent out a quote and want to be sure you hear back from the person you've sent it to.

Do you have bills you want to remind yourself to pay, or people you need to remind yourself to contact?

Throw away those paper scraps. You have two wonderful features to call upon.

Tasks and Flags

Tasks are only available in Outlook, and **Flags** in both Outlook and Outlook Express.

Tasks

The official definition of a **Task** is: a personal or work-related duty or errand that you want to track through completion.

You are going to love **Tasks**. It is one of my favourite tools in Outlook. However, the only drawback is that they rely upon **YOU** for action! And it's easy when you're busy to ignore your Tasks and let them build up. But then again, so do those scraps of paper.

Think of Tasks as your automated To Do list!

Once you create a Task, on the appointed day and at the appointed time, a small box will open on your Outlook screen telling you the Task is due. Ditto for Flags (explained next). Outlook must be open for the Task to activate.

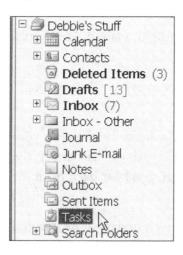

Figure 1 *Tasks live below your Sent Items folder.*

If you have an older version of Microsoft® Office (2000 and earlier) each Task due opens its own window, so to close them you have to click each individual one. With the 2002 and 2003 versions, the Tasks are amalgamated together in one pop-up window (along with Flags and Calendar items). They will stay active for a designated time period – showing up in the window each day, and every time you open Outlook. Once they're very old, they don't pop up to remind you, but they do stay in your Tasks folder, with the text turned red.

Once you start using Tasks, you'll wonder how you have lived without this function!

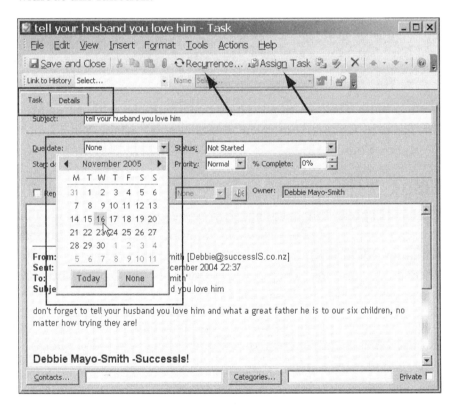

Figure 2 *A Task allows you to set when the due date is, to assign it to someone else to complete, to make it reoccur, and to track activity on it to completion.*

HOW DO I CREATE A TASK FROM SCRATCH?

1. Go to your **Tasks** Folder, and click the **New** button

or While you're anywhere in Outlook go to the **File** menu, point
to **New** and Click **Task**.

2. In the **Subject** box, type a **Task** name. Complete any other
boxes on the **Task** and **Details** tabs with information you want
to record for the **Task**.

3. To make the **Task** recur, click **Recurrence**, and click the
frequency (**Daily, Weekly, Monthly, Yearly**) at which you
want the task to recur.

Top Tip
You can drag & drop an email into the Task folder. It will open a new
Task with the original email inside.

We'll discuss Tasks in more detail along with clever business uses
for Tasks in Chapter Fourteen, in Section III: Make Your Inbox
Work For Your Business.

Flags

Outlook Express only has Flags. If you use Outlook you'd consider
using a Flag instead of a Task when you want to quickly set a simple
reminder (it's a click). In Outlook 2003 Flags have the added feature
of six colour options. Then test your memory on what importance
you have placed on each colour!

Flags are based on an existing item, an email, or a contact, for
example. Tasks can be created new and can be stand-alone items.

Top Tip
Microsoft Tutorial Online – Flags:
http://office.microsoft.com/training/Training.aspx?AssetID=RP01115
5981033&CTT=6&Origin=RC011156011033

Prior to Microsoft® Office 2003

HOW DO I ADD FLAGS TO EMAILS?

1. When composing an email, click the **Flag** button (right-click the email and select the red flag).
2. The **Flag For Follow Up** dialogue box opens.
3. Select an action to display across top of email from the **Flag To** drop-down menu.
4. Chose a date from the **Due By** drop-down calendar, using the arrows to navigate to another month or year. By default, **5:00 PM** on the target date is displayed; you can click into the field and change the time.

> **Top Tip**
> Add your own words to a follow-up flag for a new email.
>
> Click the **Message Flag** button and then type the text you want in the **Flag to** box.

Microsoft® Office 2003

HOW DO I ADD A FLAG TO AN EMAIL?

1. Find an email you would like to **Flag** in your Inbox.
2. Right-click the **Flag Status** column for the email and select the colour **Flag** you desire.

HOW DO I REMOVE OR ALTER A FLAG?

1. Right-click on the email; a pop-up menu displays.
2. Select one of the following options:
   - **Flag Complete** to turn the flag white, indicating you are finished.
   - **Clear Flag** to remove the flag.

Figure 3 *Create a Flag by right-clicking an existing email or selecting the Flag icon when you're writing a new email.*

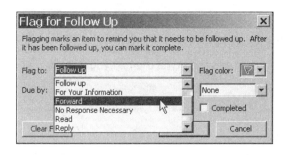

Figure 4 *Flags can be given instructions.*

HOW DO I ADD A FLAG TO AN OPEN EMAIL?

When you open an email to read it, you may want to attach a Flag to it right then and there. Here's how you would do that.

1. Double-click an email in the **Inbox** to open it if you're looking at it in **Preview**.

2. On the **Standard** toolbar, click the **Follow Up** button (a little red flag icon).

3. Click the **Flag color** drop-down arrow, select a **Flag**, and click **OK**.

4. Click the **Close** button to close the email.

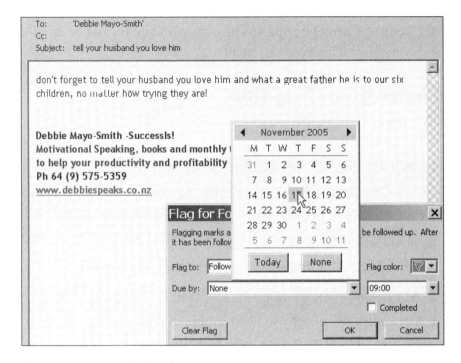

Figure 5 *Flags can be dated.*

Top Tip

Jog your memory with a follow-up Flag.

Create a follow-up Flag as a reminder to follow up on an email. On the **Actions** menu, click **Follow Up** and click the flag colour of your choice.

HOW DO I ADD A REMINDER?

1. Right-click the **Flag Status** column for an email and click **Add Reminder**.

2. The **Flag for Follow Up** dialogue box is displayed. Choose what you want and click OK.

3. If you wanted to receive a reminder to follow up on this email, you would click the **Due By** drop-down arrow and select a date. You could specify a time in the next box to the right.

4. Click the **Cancel** button to close the dialogue box without saving any changes to the email.

4 More great Flag tips
How do I ...

1. QUICKLY CHANGE THE COLOUR OF A FLAG? (OUTLOOK 2003)

Locate the flagged email in the email list. Right-click the flag, and then click the Flag colour that you want on the shortcut menu.

2. FLAG THAT EMAIL FAST?

Select an email in the email list, and then press INSERT.

3. SET A REMINDER TO REPLY TO AN EMAIL?

a. Right-click the email you want to set the reminder for, point to **Follow Up** and then click **Add Reminder**.

b. In the **Due By list**, click the date when you have to complete the reply.

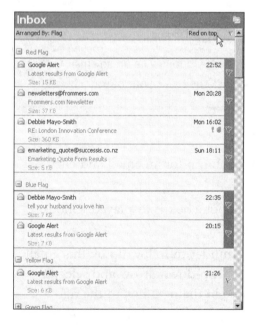

Figure 6 *Arranging your emails by Flags.*

c. In the second list, click a time.

d. In the Flag colour list, click the flag colour you want, and then click **OK**.

4. HOW DO I SORT EMAILS ACCORDING TO THEIR FLAGS?

Want to see all of the flags together? That's easy.

a. Point to **Arrange By** on the **View** menu.

b. **Tip:** Write down the menu command that is currently selected so that you can return to it when you've finished viewing emails by flag.

c. On the **Arrange By** submenu, click **Flag**. Your emails should now be sorted according to the flags that you've assigned them.

d. Restore your old Inbox arrangement by pointing to **Arrange By** on the **View** menu and clicking the arrangement you noted in Step 4b.

CHAPTER SIX

Help! I waste so much time mucking around with my emails

Solutions in this chapter

- ☑ Using **My Shortcuts**
- ☑ Innovate your use of drag & drop
- ☑ Fast-track with right-clicking
- ☑ Smart uses for the 2002 and 2003 **clipboards**
- ☑ Great **Keyboard Shortcuts** you must know

Understanding shortcuts

When I interview potential employees, I sit them down at the computer, sit next to them, and ask them to do several easy-to-intermediate computer tasks.

I'll start them in **Word**, typing something in. We move on to **Excel** (my favourite program – but that's another book *Superb Tips and Tricks For Managing Your Customer Information* www.successis.co.nz/books.htm). Then we go into **Outlook**.

I don't care about their speed of typing. I look for how many shortcuts they use. Do they know a keyboard shortcut instead of going to the drop-down menu and selecting it there? Do they know different functions, or do they do things manually?

Why is it so important to me? Because the more shortcuts and tricks they use, the more productive our office is. And to be frank, the lower my administration costs are. Wouldn't you like to get more done in less time?

Top Tip

Use drag & drop to copy, too.

When you drag & drop in or outside of Outlook (such as moving a Word document from one folder to another while in Windows® Explorer), if you hold down the Control key at the same time, it creates a copy where you drop, leaving the original intact. If you don't hold down the Control key, it will move it instead of copying.

Your learning is magnified

What you learn in these chapters – as well as the keyboard shortcuts in Appendix III – works across **ALL** your Microsoft® software: Word, Excel, Access and Publisher as well as Outlook and Outlook Express.

Drag & drop

A lovely feature that is so easy to overlook, or not be creative with, is drag & drop. You're probably familiar with it when you move an email into a folder. But experiment! One of my favourite drag & drop shortcuts (see Chapter 17) I found completely by accident.

Top Tip

Here's a super business drag & drop tip.

Have a group of people you want to email? If you have their contact details in a column (such as an Excel column, Access column or a table in Word), you can highlight the entire column of email addresses, copy and paste them straight into the To, Cc, or Bcc address field of your outgoing email.

Drag & drop saves you time by not having to click, use drop-down menus, copy or paste. You can take an email and, while selected with the mouse, drag it and drop it where you want. The original email will still remain where it was.

The beauty of this is that all the information in that email is copied in the text box of the new item. For example, you can take an email and drag & drop it into your Tasks folder – that email will open up as a new Task. Same for Contacts. Same for Calendar.

Top Tip

In business, you might want to move contact details from an email into your database.

You can have the email open on half the screen, then have your Excel or Access database open on the other half of the screen at the same time (in other words, they're both minimised to fit). You can use the highlight, drag & drop technique here too – from the email straight into your database.

Top Tip

Quickly add an attachment to a new email.

Locate the file (for example, a .doc file in your My Documents folder) and then drag it to your Inbox. Outlook opens a new email with the file attached. You can also drag multiple files.

What does the Shortcut menu in Outlook do?

It's easy to overlook what you see every day but don't take the time to explore!

I'm Criminal with this

It was like that with me. I never noticed or used My Shortcuts until I saw them in my husband's Outlook. Basically, My Shortcuts are links you create to anything you want. A web page. One of your folders in Outlook. A Word document. The official Microsoft® definition (if you don't care for my loosely worded one) is: an icon and associated name in the Shortcuts pane that offers quick access to a folder.

My Shortcuts

You can create your own shortcuts and remove existing ones in each group. When you click on the shortcut, it will open your selection in a new window if it's a folder from your documents (as in Figure 2). Otherwise it will open in Outlook.

HOW DO I ADD A SHORTCUT?

1. On the **Go** menu, click **Shortcuts**.

2. In the **Shortcuts** pane in the **Navigation Pane**, click **Add New Shortcut**.

3. In the **Add to Navigation Pane** dialogue box, click the folder you want to create a shortcut for.

4. Click **OK**.

Figure 1 *You'll find Shortcuts in the Navigation Pane. Here's an example with the 2003 Navigation Pane.*

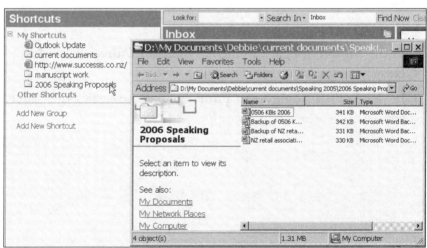

Figure 2 *Selecting my shortcut folder '2006 Speaking Proposals' results in a new window, opening the Windows® Explorer program at just the right spot.*

> **Top Tip**
>
> Don't forget our new friend drag & drop!
>
> Look at Figure 2. If I took my mouse and dragged the file 0506 KBis 2006 from Windows® Explorer to Shortcuts in Outlook and dropped it there, it would create a link.

New shortcuts are added to the first **Shortcut Group**. If you want the shortcut in another group, click the shortcut you added, and then drag it to the shortcut group you want.

Do you right-click?

You'd be surprised by all the things you can do in all the different programs of Microsoft® Office when you right-click your mouse!

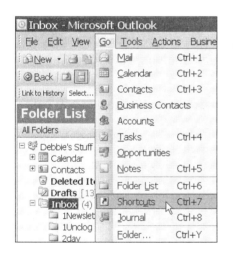

Figure 3 *If you normally work in folder view like I do, you'd never know Shortcuts exist. Perhaps, like me, you might not have noticed that little 'Go' menu either, or explored it.*

Options available when you right-click an email in Outlook

Note, this menu is similar for Outlook 2000, 2002 and 2003. Only Outlook 2003 has the new **Create Rule** option (see point 11).

1. **Open** – opens the selected email.

2. **Print** – sends the selected email to a printer.

3. **Reply** – opens an email pre-addressed to the sender of the original email, with the original email still intact.

4. **Reply to All** – opens a new email pre-addressed to the original sender, plus all recipients of the email, with the original email still intact.

5. **Forward** – opens a new email, with the original email intact, and you must specify recipients.

6. **View Attachments** (not in 2003) – displays a submenu of the attachments' filenames; when one is selected your computer opens the file in an appropriate application.

7. **Follow Up** (2003) / **Flag for Follow Up** (prior to 2003) – opens the **Flag for Follow Up** dialogue box, and allows you to select follow-up options and due dates.

8. **Mark as Unread** – displays the closed envelope icon and changes the text to boldface so the email appears to be unread.

9. **Categories** – opens the **Categories** dialogue box so you can assign a category to the email.

10. **Find All** – displays a submenu so you can select options to refine the search for emails:

    Related Messages – searches the folder by subject line.

    Messages from Sender – searches the folder by the sender's name.

11. **Create Rule** (new in 2003) – you can create a new rule from that email.

12. **Junk E-mail** – displays a submenu allowing you to select options to add the email to a junk sender's list, if you have used the **Organizer** to turn on filtering of junk email. The list options are:

Add to Junk Senders list.

Add to Adult Content Senders list.

Figure 4 *Right-clicking Outlook.*

13. **Delete** – moves the email to the **Deleted Items** folder.

14. **Move to Folder** – opens the **Move Items** dialogue box and allows you to select the destination folder for storage of the email.

15. **Options** – opens the Message Options dialogue box.

Options available with Outlook Express right-click

The options are much more limited than with Outlook.

- **Reply to Sender** is the same as **Reply** in Outlook.

- **Forward** and **Forward As Attachment** differ as **Forward** opens a new email with the original email intact and you must specify recipients. **Forward as Attachment** creates a new message, with the selected message as an attachment.

- **Copy to Folder** copies the email to the folder you select while leaving the original intact. This contrasts with the **Move to Folder** option in Outlook.

- **Add Sender to Address Book** This adds the Sender of the the selected message to your address book

- **Properties** This displays the properties of the selected items (such as date, from whom, size of file).

Figure 5 *Right-clicking Outlook Express.*

New 2002 and 2003 clipboard

One of the improvements in the 2002 and 2003 software is the ability of the clipboard to hold in memory the last 24 things you have copied. It doesn't matter if you've gone from Outlook to Word to Excel and back again. The clipboard holds all the different things you've copied in the programs. It also allows you to paste between programs.

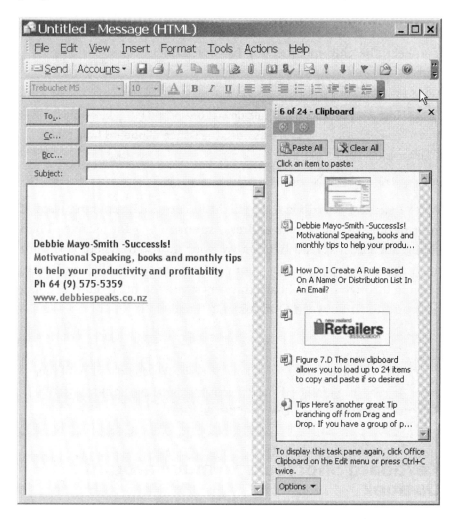

Figure 6 *The new clipboard allows you to load up to 24 items to copy and paste. Here's the Office Clipboard opened with a new email. Anything (and everything) in the clipboard can be pasted into that email.*

You can ignore that feature – or put it to good use

Here's a good time-saving example. Let's say contact information you need to store elsewhere comes in via five emails. Perhaps it is the contact details for five new members of a club you belong to. You keep the club membership list in Excel.

Top Tip
To open your clipboard, hold down Control and hit 'C' twice quickly (CTRL+CC). Or you can always open the **Office Clipboard** from the **Edit** menu.

What I suggest you do is to highlight in turn each separate piece of information (name, street address, suburb . . .) for all five. Then open your Excel spreadsheet, move your mouse to where you want the first new detail, select the clipboard item and then click on **Paste**. Moving through the clipboard this way saves you the tedium of going back and forth between Outlook and Excel.

Top Tip
Microsoft online tutorial on how to use the keyboard instead of your mouse: http://office.microsoft.com/training/Training.aspx?AssetID=RC010393301033&CTT=6&Origin=RC010393301033

Keyboard Shortcuts to move around Outlook

- Press CTRL+1 for Mail.
- Press CTRL+2 for Calendar.
- Press CTRL+3 for Contacts.
- Press CTRL+4 for Tasks.
- Press CTRL+5 for Notes.
- Press CTRL+6 for Folder List.
- Press CTRL+7 for Shortcuts.

Common Keyboard Shortcuts you should know and love

ACTION	KEYBOARD SHORTCUT
Open	CTRL+O
Undo	CTRL+Z
Redo. In some programs, if there is nothing to redo, this repeats the last action	CTRL+Y
Save	CTRL+S
Print	CTRL+P
Close the active window	ALT+F4
Bold	CTRL+B
Italic	CTRL+I
Underline	CTRL+U
Align right	CTRL+R
Align centre	CTRL+E
Align left	CTRL+L
Copy	CTRL+C
Cut	CTRL+X
Paste	CTRL+V
Open the clipboard	CTRL+C+C
Find	CTRL+F
Replace	CTRL+H
Select whole document	CTRL+A
Spell checker	F7
Thesaurus	SHIFT+F7
Style box	CTRL+SHIFT+S
Font	CTRL+SHIFT+F
Change font to Normal style	CTRL+SHIFT+N

Top Tip

There's a great explanation in Appendix I, showing how to switch the focus from clicking your mouse to the menu bar. It's hitting ALT and then the underlined letter in the menu.

So, for example, to open something – instead of Clicking Open with the mouse, or CTRL+O as above, you would Select ALT+F (File menu), then hit O (for Open)

CHAPTER SEVEN

Help!
How do I make it easier for people to get back to me?

Signatures

Did you know that you can automatically 'sign' each email you send? By that I don't mean an actual signature of your name, but your contact details. (Actually you *could* include a graphic of your signature, but why on earth would you want to?)

At least include your telephone number and your name. Why? What do you think is always in close proximity to most computers? Telephones.

When you send an email that requires action, you want to make it as easy as can be for someone to get back to you – don't you? Don't make them hunt around for your contact details! Give it to them at the bottom of your email.

If you use your computer for home and business use, you can have different signatures for each use. In fact, be **smart** about signatures. **Make them work for you! Here are some examples:**

- Marketing specials of the week/month.
- Different signatures to different customer groups.
- Offer subscriptions to your newsletter.
- Send them to your website.

Just don't go overboard and make your signatures too long! Name, title, company, address, phone, web address. It's not necessary to put your email address. They'll have that on hitting reply.

OUTLOOK: HOW DO I AUTOMATICALLY INSERT A SIGNATURE IN ALL NEW EMAILS, OR IN ALL EMAILS I REPLY TO OR FORWARD?

1. From the main Microsoft® Outlook window, on the **Tools** menu, click **Options** and click the **Mail Format** tab.

2. In the **Compose in this message format** list, click the email format that you want to use the signature with (HTML, Rich Text or Plain Text.)

3. Under **Signature**, select an email account. If this is your first signature or you want to do a new one, click **New**. Otherwise choose the signatures you want to use for new email and for replies and forwards. **You can use different signatures for each**.

HOW DO I MANUALLY INSERT A SIGNATURE IN AN INDIVIDUAL EMAIL?

(This feature is not available if you are using Microsoft® Word as your email editor.)

1. Create or open the email.

2. In the email body, click where you want to insert the signature.

3. On the **Insert** menu, point to **Signature**, and then click the signature you want.

If the signature you want is not listed, click **More**, and in the **Signature** box, select the one you want to use.

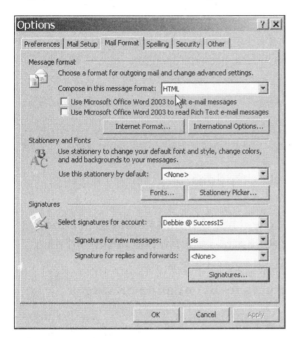

Figure 1 *You get to Signatures in Outlook via Tools > Options > Mail Format > Signature.*

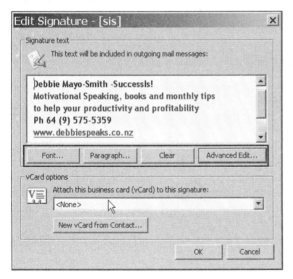

Figure 2 *Your signatures don't have to be Plain Janes! You can select the edit button to add hyperlinks, images, formatting, and more.*

Top Tip

You can attach your contact details to your signature in the form of a vCard (as shown in Figure 2).

All the recipient has to do is click on it and it will add you straight into their contacts. A vCard is the Internet standard for creating and sharing virtual business cards.

OUTLOOK EXPRESS: HOW DO I ADD A SIGNATURE TO OUTGOING EMAILS?

1. On the **Tools** menu, click **Options**, and then click the **Signatures** tab.

2. To create a signature, click the **New** button and then either enter text in the **Edit Signature** box, or click **File** and then find the text or HTML file you'd like to use.

3. Select the **Add signatures to all outgoing messages** check box.

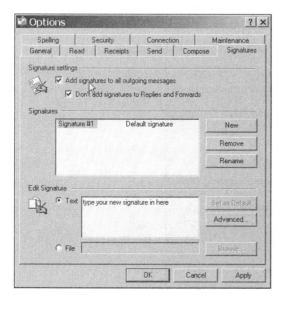

Figure 3 *Tools > Options > Signatures is where you'll find your Outlook Express signature settings.*

Be sure to make your web addresses work!

Often, just typing in www.yourcompany or you@youraddress in your signature will *not* mean that the recipient can click on it to take them to your website, or open a new email to you.

You must actively create these hyperlinks. Even though the Microsoft® signature instructions tell you that you don't have to (and I quote: 'If the URL begins with www, you can leave off the http:// designation. Microsoft Outlook will automatically format the URL as a link to the Web') you **should!** If your email goes to someone who isn't on Outlook/Outlook Express or who only opts to have plain text emails, they might not be able to click on your email or web address and make it work.

Just get in the habit when creating your signature (or typing things in manually in your emails) to always:

- Preface your web addresses with **http://**
  http://www.yourcompany
- Preface email addresses with **mailto:**
  mailto:yourname@yourcompany

Always be sure to use this code when you are creating your emails in the professional web software like Dreamweaver or FrontPage.

> **Top Tip**
>
> Hide email/web addresses behind text. For example, you can add 'Visit our website' to your email signature, and have that text hyperlinked to the much longer unfriendly URL of a web page.
>
> To do this, simply select **Advanced Edit** when creating your signature – it will open up Word or Front Page as your email editor and help you to set it up.

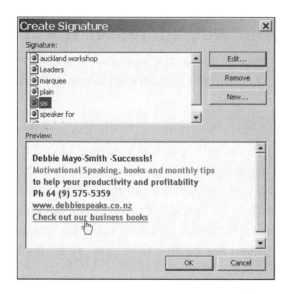

Figure 4 *You can hide web addresses under text. Here, if someone clicked on the words 'Check out our business books' it would open the web page* **http:// www.successis.co.nz/ books.htm**

The From Address line

Do you have someone using your computer temporarily? Do you go on the road or out of the office and have an assistant open and reply to your emails? If they send an email, it appears as if it's coming from you.

You can change that. If the assistant has their own email address, they can let the recipient know it's from them on behalf of you (and not you personally). This works through something called the **From Address** line.

HOW CAN I GET THE FROM ADDRESS LINE TO SHOW?

1. Open a **New** email
2. Select **View** menu
3. Select **From Field**.

If it's not in your View menu, it will be in the Options menu (as shown in Figure 5).

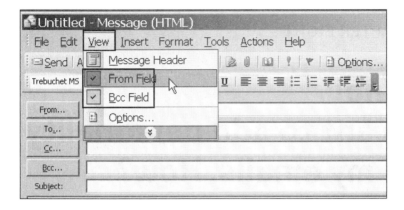

Figure 5 *If someone is using your Outlook, you might not want the recipient to think the email they sent is from you. The From Field allows their email address to be loaded so the recipient knows who it's from.*

Top Tip

What on earth is Cc and Bcc?

Cc is shorthand for Carbon copy. Remember those blue carbon papers you used to use with typewriters to make two copies? If you add a recipient's name to the Cc box in an email, a copy of the email is sent to that recipient, and the recipient's name is visible to other recipients of the email.

Bcc is shorthand for Blind carbon copy. If you add a recipient's name to this box in an email, a copy of the email is sent to that recipient, but the recipient's name is **not** visible to other recipients of the email. If the **Bcc** box isn't visible when you create a new email, you can add it as above in Figure 5 by selecting **Bcc Field** from the **View** menu.

CHAPTER EIGHT

Help!
I want to add personality
to my emails. How?

Solutions in this chapter

☑ Dress up your emails with **Stationery**

☑ Forget Typewriter, say hello to colour and style with
HTML

Dressing up your emails

Your options are enormous when it comes to dressing up your
emails. From changing fonts, to adding a graphic, to changing the
entire background with stationery templates. Even designing your
own from scratch!

The bottom line is: do you want to do the stationery bit for everyday
emails? More on this later – I don't want to be a killjoy right off the
bat.

Your options:

- You have 22 stationery background templates loaded in
  Outlook; 13 in Outlook Express.

- There are 8 more on the Microsoft® website. Wait until you
  try to type this address in:

http://office.microsoft.com/en-au/officeupdate/CD010225931 033.aspx?DPC=%7BCC29EA4B-7BC2-11D1-A921-00A0C 91E2AA2%7D&DCC=%7BE913BCD4-9560-11D1-87C1-0 0AA00A71E2D%7D&AppName=Microsoft%20Outlook&clc id=0x0409&HelpLCID=0x0409 (or try doing a search in the Microsoft Website for Outlook Stationery templates.)

- You can edit any of the templates.
- You can create your own from scratch using your own graphics and design.
- You can change your type face (font), its size and colour.

Before we begin

Go to Chapter Eleven for a full description of the different types of email you can send. For now I'll list the **three types of email:**

1. **Plain text** (typewriter).
2. **Rich Text** (formatting and colour).
3. **HTML** (formatting, colour and embedded graphics/pictures/ images).

Figure 1 *You can scroll through the selections of stationery backgrounds and select which one tickles your fancy. This is the Jungle look.*

To use Stationery or to use any font other than the plain text standard Courier, you'll need to have your email default set to send as HTML.

OUTLOOK: HOW DO I TURN HTML ON?

1. From the main Outlook window, on the **Tools** menu, click **Options** and click the **Mail Format** tab.

2. Select HTML.

OUTLOOK EXPRESS: HOW DO I TURN HTML ON?

1. From the main Outlook window, on the **Tools** menu, click **Options** and click the **Send** tab.

2. Select HTML.

Stationery Templates

OUTLOOK: HOW DO I USE EXISTING STATIONERY TEMPLATES?

1. From the main Outlook window, on the **Tools** menu, click **Options**, and click the **Mail Format** tab.

2. Click **Stationery Picker** and choose a template.

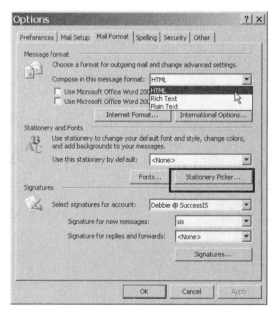

Figure 2 *Turning on your HTML option for outgoing emails in Outlook. Stationery Picker is right below it.*

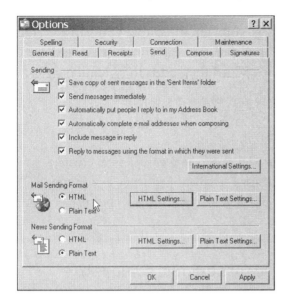

Figure 3 *Turning on your HTML option for outgoing emails in Outlook Express.*

OUTLOOK: HOW DO I CREATE STATIONERY?

(Remember stationery is available only if you use HTML as your email format.)

1. From the main Outlook window, on the **Tools** menu, click **Options** and click the **Mail Format** tab.

2. Click **Stationery Picker**.

3. Click **New**.

4. In the **Enter a name for your new stationery** box, enter a name.

5. Under **Choose how to create your stationery**, select the option you want.

6. To select a file to base your stationery on, type the path and file name in the **Use this file as a template** box, or click **Browse** to select from a list.

7. Click **Next**.

8. Select the options you want to use.

Note: If Microsoft® Word is your email editor, you can't create new stationery from Word. However, you can create a new stationery in Microsoft® Outlook, which Word then adds to its stationery list.

Top Tip

Beware dark backgrounds.

They make it very hard for your text to be seen, unless you change your font colour to white or similar. Even then, if someone forwards on your email, their email will be probably in blue and again, unreadable against a dark background.

OUTLOOK EXPRESS: HOW DO I USE EXISTING STATIONERY TEMPLATES?

1. On the **Tools** menu, click **Options** and click the **Compose** tab.

2. In the **Stationery** area, make sure is checked, and then select the one you want.

3. Hit **Select**

OUTLOOK EXPRESS: HOW DO I CREATE STATIONERY?

1. On the **Tools** menu, click **Options** and click the **Compose** tab.

2. In the **Stationery** area, and then click **Create New**.

Clever ideas
Problems to consider when using Stationery

Stationery is great for friends. For doing a party or an event invitation. For something festive or different. Personally, for business I never have, and never will, use stationery. I only use signatures. Why?

1. It automatically turns your email into an HTML one. A big problem for people on plain text. They'll have to open your email in Internet Explorer or it loses all the coding.

2. Not everyone has the ability to view graphics or pictures. So if you have your picture or a company logo embedded, they'll have to open your email with Internet Explorer (or similar web program). Also, people who are on Lotus Notes will see any images as paper clip attachments, not embedded in your stationery.

3. Let's face it. In business, you (and your company) are the only ones that care about your branding, your logo. Not the recipient.

4. Stationery can add a lot of weight onto the email, making it slower to download.

5. Dark backgrounds and busy backgrounds can make the text from someone replying to you or forwarding it on others very difficult to read.

6. For business, most stationaries are not professional-looking.

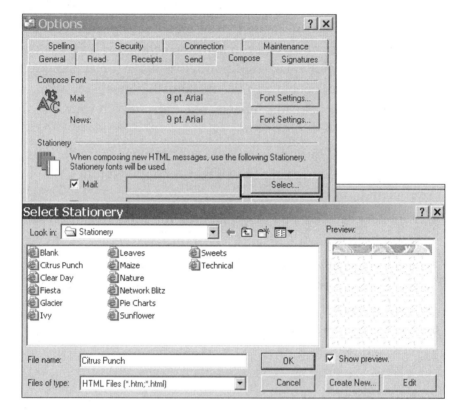

Figure 4 *Outlook Express stationery is accessed through Tools > Options > Compose > Stationery > Select.*

Let your type speak for you

Ever notice how fonts have personality? From the happy, smiley-feeling Comic Sans to the art deco **Britannic Bold,** you can add a bit more personality to your emails.

You must know by now that you can change the font whenever you like in an email. Remember your email format needs to be set to HTML. You select the text you've written, then on the **Format** menu select **Font.**

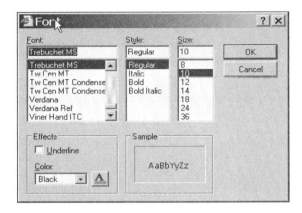

Figure 5 *You can change the font of any text you type in by selecting **Font** on the Format menu. This dialogue box opens. You can also set a default font.*

Your own default

You can also set the font, font colour and the size you want as the default for each new email you create.

HOW DO I CHANGE MY DEFAULT FONT FOR NEW, FORWARDED, AND REPLIED TO EMAILS?

1. From the main Microsoft® Outlook window, on the **Tools** menu, click **Options**, then click the **Mail Format** tab.

2. Click **Fonts**.

3. Choose the font you want. My favourite is **Trebuchet**.

Remember to set your email format to HTML.

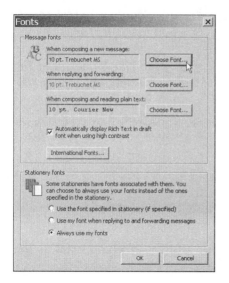

Figure 6 *Instead of selecting stationery, why not change your font? You can choose the type, size and colour.*

Two important points to consider with fonts

Different fonts for different folks

The first is that not all computers have the same fonts. People on Apple Mac computers will have different ones to people on PCs. Not all PCs have all the fonts.

So, it's best practice to use common ones. If you use a font for your email that is not installed in the recipient's computer, it will change to that computer's default font.

Standard fonts are Tahoma, Arial, Verdana, Times Roman and Helvetica. Let's not forget the plain text standard around the world: Courier.

Fonts speak

Second, and equally important, is that the content of your 'message' may not match the character of your font. I'll never forgot when I received an email about the necessity for trauma insurance – and the typeface was **Comic Sans**. It was just *wrong*. So if you often write serious emails, don't use that font.

CHAPTER NINE

Help!
How can I let people know when I'm away?

Solutions in this chapter

☑ Rules

☑ Out of Office Assistant

☑ Your ISP (Internet Service Provider)

You're going away!

Lucky you. In this day and age of always being 'wired', it's nice to have a break away from your computer and emails, isn't it? But while you might be delighting in a vacation in Fiji, or on the road travelling with limited connection – those emails can be piling up, people wondering why you haven't got back to them. So how do you let people know you're away?

Three ways:
 1. **Rules**.

 2. **Out of Office Assistant** (Networked computers only).

 3. **ISPs** (Internet Service Providers).

1. Rules (best when someone can watch over your computer)

You can use Rules to create an 'out of office' reply for emails coming in, and to look for important email addresses or words and forward a copy of the email on to a colleague to take care of.

Before I go any further though, for Rules to work you have to have your computer turned on, Outlook open and running, and be connected to the Internet. That's not something I would relish if I were going away on vacation. But if you're part of a small office, this is ideal. Either your computer would be receiving emails anyway, or someone can crank that baby up for you once a day.

SO HOW DO I LET PEOPLE KNOW I'M AWAY?

Create your own email template to go with a Rule advising you're away from home or the office.

First step – creating your Away/On Vacation message

1. First open a new and blank email (CTRL+N).
2. Type in your vacation message and the subject line.
3. Save that email by selecting **File, Save As**.
4. Click the bottom drop down menu and Select **Outlook Template**.

Next step – set up the Rule

1. Go to **Tools**. Select **Rules and Alerts**.
2. Select **New Rule**.
3. Select **Start from a Blank Rule**.
4. I suggest you select **Check Messages** 'When emails arrive', and then proceed to the next step where my name appears in the **To** box.
5. I suggest you then select **Reply using a specific template**.
6. If you don't see your new email under **Standard Templates**,

click the drop-down menu (Figure 1) and find yours in the **User Templates** in **File System**.

7. Finish with any additions and exceptions you desire.

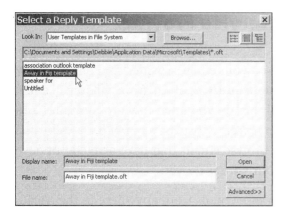

Figure 1 *As described in setting up a Rule, you can create email templates and then set up Rules to automatically send them.*

2. Networked system

If you're on a networked system with Microsoft® Exchange or SharePoint, you'll have an Out of Office Assistant to help you with everything (and I'm sure you know all about it already).

HOW DO I TURN ON MY OUT OF OFFICE ASSISTANT?

1. On the **Tools** menu, click **Out of Office Assistant**.

2. Click **Add Rule**.

3. Under **When a message arrives that meets the following conditions**, specify the conditions of the rule that the message must meet for the action to occur.

4. To specify more conditions, click **Advanced**, select the options you want, and then click **OK**.

5. To specify that this rule must be the last one applied, select the **Do not process subsequent rules** check box.

6. Under **Perform these actions**, select the options you want. You can select more than one option.

Note: If you specify that an email must be deleted, rules that come after this delete rule in the list of rules in the **Out of Office Assistant** dialogue box do not affect the email.

3. Your Internet Service Provider

If your email system is set up using Post Office Protocol 3 (POP3), your email is initially stored on your email provider's server. But once you go and 'get it' (clicking **Send/Receive**) from whatever email program you use, the emails are downloaded to your computer and are no longer stored on the server. Most ISPs today have web-mail functions that allow you to browse emails that have arrived but have not been downloaded to your computer yet.

Besides being able to view these emails from anywhere in the world, you can also work with these emails. Reply to them, send new ones, and (of course) create rules. Two things to be aware of are one, when you send emails from the web, you need to save a **Sent Copy** or **Blind Carbon Copy** yourself; and two, that you normally have a size limit to your mailbox and the emails you send as web mail will not get downloaded to your computer automatically.

While the instructions will be different for each ISP, under **Options** and then **Rules** you should find the capability to set up automatic vacation emails to advise colleagues, friends and family when you are out of the office or away from home.

CHAPTER TEN

Help! Any more time-saving tips?

Solutions in this chapter

☑ 15 more great time-saving email tips

---

15 more great time-saving email tips
How do I . . .

---

1. RECALL THAT EMAIL (Outlook)?

To recall or replace a sent email, open the email in the Sent Items folder, and on the **Actions** menu, click **Recall This Message**. Only ones that haven't been read yet can be retrieved.

2. FIND RELATED EMAILS?

To find related emails, right-click the email. Then on the **Shortcut** menu, point to **Find All** and then click **Related Messages**. The **Advanced Find** dialogue box appears with a list of related emails.

3. KNOW WHEN PEOPLE HAVE READ MY EMAILS?

On the **Tools** menu, click **Options**, and then click the **Preferences** tab. Click **Email Options**, and then click **Tracking Options** and choose.

4. VERIFY THAT THE EMAIL I RECEIVE IS AUTHENTIC?

If you have security set up, you can verify that an email you receive with a digital signature has not been tampered with. In the email, click the **Verify Digital Signature** button.

5. SEE MORE EMAILS IN MY INBOX?

a. Change from multi-line view to single-line view. On the **View** menu, point to **Arrange By,** and then click **Custom**. Click **Other Settings**.

b. Clear the **Use multi-line layout in widths smaller than *n* characters** check box.

6. QUICKLY TEST THE HYPERLINK IN THE EMAIL I JUST WROTE?

Press CTRL while you click the hyperlink.

7. CHOOSE WHICH EMAIL ACCOUNT TO USE?

If you have multiple email accounts set up in Outlook, you can choose which to use when sending emails. For example, you might have two domain names with email addresses, a Hotmail account and an email with your ISP. In a new email, click **Accounts,** and then click the account you want from the list.

8. DELETE NAMES FROM THE AUTOCOMPLETE LIST?

Select the unwanted name by using the UP ARROW or DOWN ARROW key and then press DELETE. Read more about this in Chapter 17.

9. SEND AN EMAIL TO MULTIPLE PEOPLE WITHOUT REVEALING OTHER RECIPIENTS' IDENTITIES?

To send an email to someone without other recipients of the email knowing, use the **Bcc** line in the email. Bcc stands for blind carbon copy. If you add someone's name to the **Bcc** line, a copy of the email is sent to that person, but his or her name is not visible to any one else.

10. MAKE SENDING A FILE THROUGH EMAIL EVEN EASIER?

You can send a file on your computer through email by right-clicking the file, pointing to **Send To**, and then clicking **Mail Recipient**. Text is automatically added to the body of the email; however, you can delete the text and add your own text by clicking in the email body and pressing CTRL+A.

11. FIND ALL EMAILS SENT BY THE SAME PERSON?

Right-click an email from that person, and then on the **Shortcut** menu, point to **Find All**. Click **Messages from Sender**. The **Advanced Find** dialogue box displays a list of all emails in a folder from that person. Don't forget you can also sort emails by who sent them to you, if you have that field showing in your Inbox.

12. SAVE MULTIPLE ATTACHMENTS AT ONE TIME?

a. Open the email. On the **File** menu, click **Save Attachments**.

b. Click **OK**, and then click the folder where you want to save the attached files. Click **OK**.

13. CREATE A RULE FROM AN EMAIL? (OUTLOOK 2003 ONLY)

a. Right-click the email, and then click **Create Rule**.

b. Select the conditions and actions you want to apply, and then click **OK**.

14. MAKE AN EMAIL UNAVAILABLE TO RECIPIENTS AFTER A SPECIFIC DATE?

a. To set the expiration date on an email you are composing, click **Options**.

b. Under **Delivery options**, select the **Expires after** check box, and then in the lists, select the date and time you want the email to expire.

15. OPEN SEVERAL EMAILS AT THE SAME TIME?

a. Hold CTRL while you click each email.

b. After you select the emails, on the **File** menu, point to **Open**, and then click **Selected Items**.

MAKE YOUR INBOX WORK FOR YOUR BUSINESS

CHAPTER ELEVEN

Help! Why do my emails to people get scrambled at the recipient's end?

Solutions in this chapter

☑ Know your email type

☑ Outlook's built-in **Sniffer**

☑ Listen to what Outlook/Outlook Express tells you – **Formatting Tool Bar**

☑ Don'ts for email marketing and newsletters

Three types of email

Before you can understand how your emails can get scrambled at the recipient's end, or don't arrive looking as you sent them, we must cover a bit of technical information.

Three types of emails:
- **Plain Text** – plain typewriter style.
- **Rich Text** – formatted text.
- **HTML** – formatted text and images.

Outlook can send and receive emails in these three formats; Outlook Express doesn't have Rich Text. What you do is select your default setting. You can also manually set each email as described in Chapter Eight.

One caveat, though

IT managers (or those in control of your business computer) can elect to have only plain text emails allowed in or out of your computer. So, no matter how many times you select HTML for your emails, if the company server is set up to send plain text only – that is what will go out.

Similarly, your recipients (though their systems can receive HTML) might have their server set up to receive plain text only.

Let's talk a bit more about what you can do (or, with plain text – what you can't do!).

HTML format

1. Text formatting (different fonts, sizes and colours).
2. Numbering.
3. Bullets.
4. Alignment (left, right and centre).
5. Horizontal lines.
6. Pictures (including backgrounds).
7. HTML styles.
8. Stationery.
9. Signatures.
10. Linking to web pages.

Plain text format

Think 'typewriter'.

Plain text format is one that *all* email programs understand. It's the universal computer language. It uses Courier, at 10 point size. You can set Outlook/Outlook Express to open emails you receive in plain text format only. You can have 'plain' signatures with plain text. However, plain text doesn't support much:

1. No bold.

2. No italic.

3. No coloured fonts.

4. No other text formatting.

5. No pictures, graphics displayed directly in the email body (although you can include them as attachments).

Rich Text format

Outlook Rich Text Format (RTF) is a Microsoft® format that only the following email programs understand: Microsoft® Exchange Client versions 5.0 and 4.0, Microsoft® Outlook 2003, Outlook 2002, Outlook 2000, Outlook 98, and Outlook 97 (probably the only reason to use RTF is inter-office communication with Microsoft® Exchange Server).

Rich Text Format supports:

1. Text formatting (different fonts, sizes and colours).

2. Bullets and numbering.

3. Alignment (left, right and centre).

4. Linked objects.

Outlook automatically converts RTF emails to HTML when you send an email to an Internet recipient, so email formatting is maintained and attachments will be received properly. Outlook also automatically formats meeting and task requests and emails with voting buttons, so these items can be properly sent intact across the Internet to other Outlook users, regardless of the default format you have set.

Top Tip

When you reply to an email, Outlook preserves the format of the email you are replying to.

If you get a plain text email in, your reply to them is in plain text even if your default is HTML.

Choosing the right format

Okay. I've got the technical. Where's the problem?

First, not everyone can (or choses to) get HTML emails. Second, computers 'see' things differently. Every computer has different software, different hardware, different server settings, different defaults set up, different fonts installed (they need to have the font you use installed to view your email with your font). The age of the computer makes a difference (HTML wasn't around with the 95 software).

OKAY, SO NOW I UNDERSTAND. WHAT CAN I DO TO GET MY MESSAGE THROUGH?

1. Change email formats.

2. Listen to Outlook (formatting tool bar) – see page 129.

3. Know about Outlook's 'sniffer' – see page 132.

4. Forward the email to yourself and switch formats before you send it to everyone. This way you'll see it the way *they* see it.

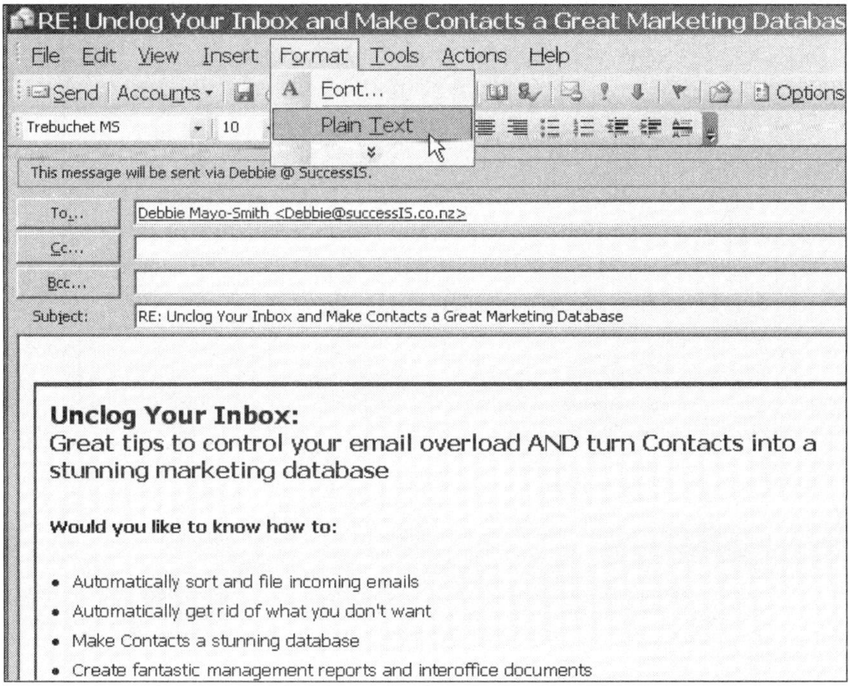

Figure 1 *When you send an individual email, you can switch it from HTML to Plain Text (or vice versa) by selecting the drop down Format menu. This is how it looks in my Inbox.*

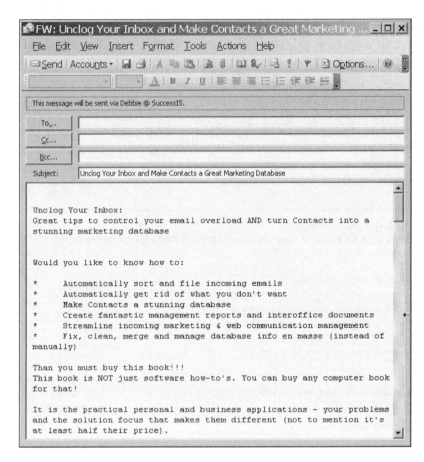

Figure 2 *The same email, converted to plain text. Outlook 2003 automatically created bullet points but prior versions might not, and other software most likely won't substitute asterisks where it sees the HTML coding for bullets. The difference isn't significant, as this email is a simple one with not much text.*

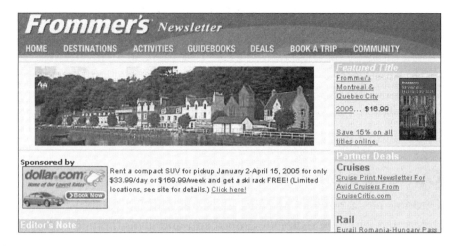

Figure 3 *Here's the 'before' picture for a normal commercial marketing email with graphics.*

Figure 4 *Look at it now in plain text. This is why if you create marketing emails it's important to have the two versions available. Most companies use professional distribution systems that send out two copies simultaneously to each recipient – the HTML and plain text. The system delivers the correct version to the recipient's computer.*

HOW DO I CHANGE EMAIL FORMATS?

1. To set your default so each new email you create is the same type, go to **Tools** then click **Options** and click on the **Mail Format** tab.

2. To change only the email you're sending, just click on the **Format** menu and select the format you want.

3. In most cases, you don't need to change the email format. When you send an HTML email to others whose mail program doesn't understand HTML, their mail program automatically displays a plain text version in the email body.

Outlook's Built-In Sniffer

Outlook has a built-in 'sniffer'. This was alluded to above. It will determine what the recipient can accept, and gives them the correct version for their computer. So if you send something in HTML and they require plain text, it converts it for you. Great news, mostly, but if you're doing any email marketing or a business communication, it won't look at all like you sent it. Remember – plain text doesn't support anything except for Courier typeface, size 10, small or capital letters. That's it. So say goodbye to your numbered or bulleted lists, different-sized fonts or headings, formatting or colour.

Don't think of pasting **Excel** spreadsheet information into an email, or text from a **Word** document where you used tabs, if you think anyone with plain text only will receive your email.

Apple Macs and Lotus Notes do funny things to emails too.

Outlook's Formatting Toolbar

Study the formatting toolbar

My advice – listen to what Outlook or Outlook Express tell you they can safely do. Look at what formatting they allow for on the toolbar (see Figure 5). That is what can be safely sent to recipients on most computers.

Top Tip

Don't take an Excel table (spreadsheet), paste it into Outlook/ Outlook Express, and send it to a large group of people.

Those on plain text, versions of Outlook prior to 2000, Apple Macs or Lotus Notes will not receive the information in separated rows and columns. They'll all disappear, and the text will be jumbled together.

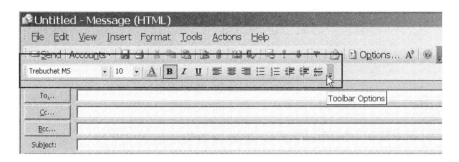

Figure 5 *Listen to what Outlook/Outlook Express is telling you.*

Don'ts for Email Marketing and Newsletters

Single web pages

Email marketing goes a step further, normally. The emails and newsletters we receive are in reality single-page web pages. Often text looks like it's in columns (it's really hidden tables), and there's background colour and images. These emails aren't created in Outlook but in web-design programs such as Macromedia Dreamweaver or Microsoft® FrontPage. Look at the difference between the Figure 1 and 2 comparison and the Figure 3 and 4 comparison.

Some people will take a Dreamweaver or FrontPage marketing email, copy it, paste it into an Outlook/Outlook Express email and send it. DON'T. Why?

Only your recipients that are on Outlook/Outlook Express year 2000 and above, *plus* have HTML selected, will see it the way it is meant to be – with the images, tables, background colour, etc. Others, such as those on Apple Macs, LotusNotes (many large corporations use Lotus Notes, an IBM program), or those on plain text, will not see it correctly.

> **Top Tip**
> Never even contemplate sending a regular **Microsoft Publisher** document. Publisher files can only be opened and read by people who have that same version of Publisher (and that's not many). If you save your Publisher document as a web page, it converts it to HTML and you're safe to send it this way.

Clever ideas!

Forward an email to yourself & switch formats

Are you planning on sending an email to a group of people (who aren't in the same office as you)?

WHY NOT SEE HOW YOUR EMAIL WILL LOOK AS PLAIN TEXT?

1. Send the email to yourself.

2. Hit Forward.

3. Select **Format, Plain Text**.

4. The computer asks you if you're sure you want to do that.

5. Say **Yes**. See how it looks now.

> **Top Tip**
> If you would like to know more about creating your own marketing emails, you can order my *Professional Online Newsletters and Emails – Exactly How To Create Your Own Book* on www.successis.co.nz/ books.htm

Newsletter in mind?

If you're planning on doing a regular, longish email communication such as a newsletter, then you should do both HTML and plain text versions. Ask people, when they subscribe, what version they prefer. Don't dazzle them with technical terms. Just ask if they want it in a plain or colourful version.

There are many professional email distribution systems available that not only will send each person on your list both the HTML and the plain text version (delivering the correct one for their computer), but will also show you the statistics of who has clicked on what web links, and who has opened up your HTML email.

CHAPTER TWELVE

Help!
How can I be sure my emails are getting through to people?

Solutions in this chapter

☑ Delivery receipts

☑ Learn about Spam Filters

Bonus: how can I 'de-junk' my

☑ Personal, business, marketing and interoffice emails

The novelty is gone

Back in 1999 when I started my online newsletter, it was unique. We were one of the first to offer 'colour' with HTML, and it has been going out faithfully month after month since that first issue. I've learnt heaps from this personal experience of doing a business newsletter all these years.

Two things are certain. Email is still an excellent form of communication for business, however it's getting so much harder not only to get your email through, but to get it read.

You've got two problems.

First is making sure as best you can that your email **REACHES** your recipient. The second is getting them to **READ** it.

If you would like expert advice on how to get your content right and relevant so people want to read your emails, and in fact look forward to them, you might like to see the book I've written about that subject. It's *Successful Email Marketing – Your Complete 'How-To' Guide*. Look for it in bookstores or online www.successis.co.nz/books.htm.

You can work on the *delivery* aspect of your email by arming yourself with the knowledge of what could prevent its delivery.

But first, there is a simple way you can try to ascertain if your email got through and got read, and that's tracking emails with delivery receipts/read replies.

How can I tell if someone has read my email?

You can track whether emails you send are delivered or read by recipients' by receiving a email notification as each email is delivered or read. The contents of the email notifications are then automatically recorded on the **Tracking** tab of the original email in your **Sent Items** folder. You can automatically move email notifications in your Inbox so they don't build up.

Outlook

HOW CAN I GET NOTIFIED ABOUT ALL EMAILS?

1. On the **Tools** menu, click **Options**.
2. Click **Preferences**.
3. Click **Email Options**.
4. Click **Tracking Options**.
5. Select the **Read receipt** or the **Delivery receipt** check box.

HOW CAN I GET NOTIFIED ABOUT A SINGLE EMAIL?

1. In the email, click **Options**.

2. Under **Voting and tracking options**, select the **Request a delivery receipt for this message** or the **Request a read receipt for this message** check box.

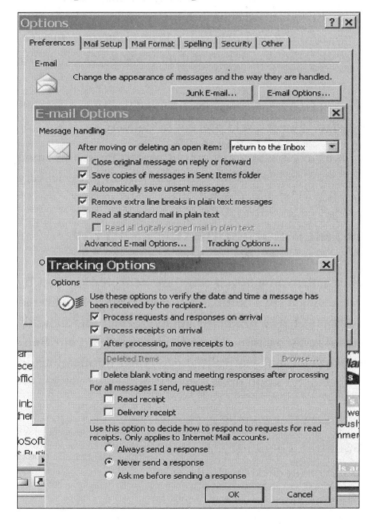

Figure 1 *Check up on important emails only by asking for a Read Receipt.*

Outlook Express

HOW CAN I GET NOTIFIED ABOUT ALL EMAILS?

1. On the **Tools** menu, click **Options**.

2. Click Receipts.

3. Select **Request a read receipt for all sent emails**.

Caveat: Read receipts don't work on all recipients' computers – and just because they receive your email doesn't mean they have to click Yes, send a reply.

Top Tip

Use Read Receipts rarely. It really bugs people.

Also be aware they can chose not to answer (I always do that) or they could be on a system that doesn't accept Read Receipts.

Moving on – what prevents delivery?
Spam filters!

Because of the problem with all that unwanted junk mail and the email viruses (see Chapter Four), for the most part now all email goes though filtering systems – from your personal emails, to your business communications, to your emails to work colleagues.

By **filtering** I mean each email is scrutinised for both the words it contains and its technical composition *before* it is delivered to the recipient.

There can be up to four levels of filtering going on!

The four levels of filtering
1. ISP (Internet Service Provider)

On your home computer and for small office systems that do not have their own server, most **Internet Service Providers (ISPs)** filter out spam, adult content and known viruses as best they can.

2. Outlook and Outlook Express junk mail

As described in Chapter Four, Outlook comes with built-in junk mail filters. Outlook Express is almost useless, as it just blocks senders.

3. Your Rules

As described in Chapter Four, people can establish their own filtering system with the Rules Wizard.

4. Business email filtering programs

The business community is handling the problem of spam by putting in strict email filters.

An email filter is a program a company buys and installs that will monitor and 'rate' incoming emails. The IT manager sets a list of what is (and is not) acceptable. Often a point-scoring system is established. Then, each incoming email is vetted by the email filter. Depending on the number of points it accrues, or whether it has forbidden content, it is either allowed in and passed on to the recipient, or is booted out. Ninety-nine per cent of the time you would not know it's not been delivered – ditto for the recipient.

Top Tip
Filter and Firewall are different.

By the way, email filters are different from firewalls and virus software. A firewall is a software program that you install which acts as a barrier between your computer and the Internet. It detects someone trying to hack into your computer. Virus software specifically looks for viruses that you might already have or blocks new ones from entering your system.

Popular firewalls such as ZoneAlarm and Sygate have free versions – suitable for home users – which you can download from their sites.

So, depending on your market and who you're going to be emailing, you'll need to know what the filters look for – especially if you have mostly business-to-business (B2B) communications. Remember, innocents can easily get caught.

Email filters are getting more sophisticated by the day. And to tell you the truth, it's at the request of the filter clients. Employers want to minimise the loss of productivity of employees.

What filters look for

Filters look at both the text and the technical composition of the email.

The words in your email

While each company sets its own protocol of what it will and won't allow, some words and phrases are universal no-no's.

- For free.
- Order today, order now.
- Money back guarantee.
- The word breast appearing without chicken within close proximity (for example).
- ! or $$$ signs appearing in the Subject line.
- Pass this email on (they look for any permutation of this).

The Outlook Junk Mail Filter

Figure 2 illustrates an example of some of the content the Microsoft® Junk Mail Filter looks for. Go to your Microsoft® Office program files and use Windows® Explorer to search for a document named **filters.txt.** You'll see exactly what your computer (and others) using Outlook considers as Junk.

The technical make-up

Have a look at the Spam Assassin list of junk mail tests. This is one of the more popular filtering programs.

http://au2.spamassassin.org/tests.html

It might seem like gobbledygook to you, but it's an extensive list of what the program looks for in the HTML coding of the email. A few examples:

- If it sees the font set at too big a size, it calls it 'shouting' and takes points away.

- If it sees non-standard font colours, it takes points away.

- It looks to see what percentage of HTML code the message has.

- It looks for 'click here'.

- It checks if something is sent Bcc (blind carbon copy).

Figure 2 *The Junk Mail Filter in Outlook – and what it screens for (yikes!).*

Bonus

HOW CAN I DE-JUNK MY PERSONAL, BUSINESS AND INTEROFFICE EMAILS?

1. Look very carefully at your text. If you've written 'only $', get rid of the 'only'. If you've written 'money back guarantee', think of a different way to word it.

2. Don't say 'forward this on to a friend' in your newsletter to get more subscribers. I just put 'New? Subscribe here' with the 'Subscribe here' hyperlinked.

3. Try to use fewer sentences with larger sized fonts.

4. Don't put punctuation such as $? ! in the subject line.

5. Forget Fr*e and trying to fool the filters. They're on to it.

6. Don't think you can put these no-no words in graphics. That's rated too – in other words, the percentage of text to graphics.

Top Tip

When people subscribe to your emails, ask them to put you on their white list, their approved list.

You might have something like this on your sign-up page: 'Our newsletter will be sent with me@mycompany in the from address. If you use a spam filter, please add this address to your approved list to ensure that you will receive the newsletter.'

Clever ideas!

Getting around Outlook 2003's ban on external links – Dramatic change for your email marketing!

As described in Chapter Four under Junk Mail Filtering, the new Outlook 2003 blocks email external links – i.e. graphics. If you haven't by now, you jolly well should redefine what your newsletters and marketing emails look like.

Click here to download pictures. To help protect your privacy, Outlook prevented automatic download of some pictures in this message.

From: Max Newmann - Editor At Large - [max.newmann@xtra.co.nz]
To: All.Xtra.customers@xtra.co.nz
Cc:
Subject: Rock, paper and scissors

Right-click here to download pictures. To help protect your privacy, Outlook prevented automatic download of this picture from the Internet.

Right-click here to download pictures. To help protect your privacy, Outlook prevented automatic download of this picture from the Internet.

Right-click here to download pictures. To help protect your privacy, Outlook prevented automatic download of this picture from the Internet.

Right-click here to download pictures. To help protect your privacy, Outlook prevented automatic download of this picture from the Internet.

Pick of the week

Right-click here to download pictures. To help protect your privacy, Outlook prevented automatic download of this picture from the Internet.

xtra.co.nz   My Profile   My Account   Help   Apple-philia

Dear Xtra customer

Right-click here to download pictures. To help protect your privacy, Outlook prevented automatic download of this picture from the Internet.

Figure 3 *Our ISP newsletter as delivered by Outlook – sans the graphics! Of course, I can right-click the email and grab the images, but nine out of ten times I don't. What do you think your email recipients would do?*

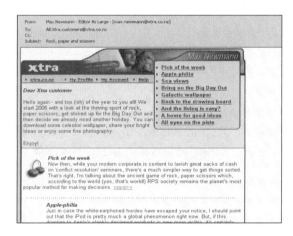

Figure 4 *What it should look like.*

Look at the example in Figure 3 from our ISP. This is how it looks in my Preview and Reading pane. Figure 4 shows what it should look like if the graphics weren't barred.

I took graphics out of my newsletter years ago (I only include them if I need to show something visually in an article). Now, I have also redesigned my newsletter to fit in with the new view in 2003. See the old versus the new in Figures 5 and 6.

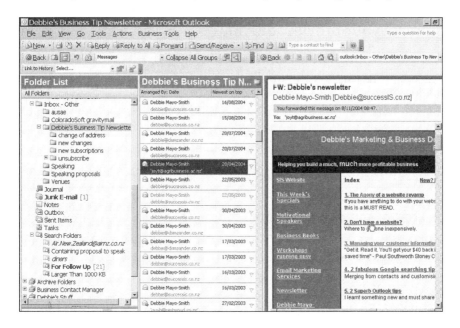

Figure 5 *Debbie's newsletter with its old design – prior to the launch of Office 2003.*

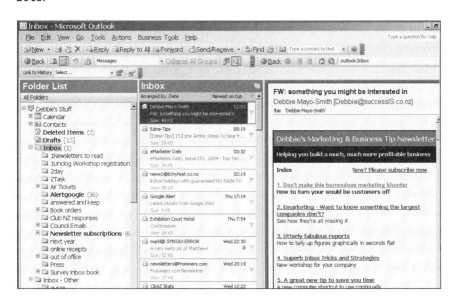

Figure 6 *Debbie's newsletter restyled to get maximum exposure in the Outlook 2003 window.*

Control your preview destiny

Remember our discussion of AutoPreview in Chapter Two? What do you notice about Figure 7?

When a recipient gets your email, they only have a few things to go on if they are just using AutoPreview. Who it's from, what the subject line says, and the first three lines of text.

You can control how your email previews by putting in the email – before anything else – a good string of keywords or a great statement instead of the normal mumbo jumbo! Figure 8 illustrates what I mean by this. It's a screenshot of my newsletter in Macromedia Dreamweaver, the software I use to create the newsletter.

The bit of text should go before anything else. The newsletter actually is all done within a table. (If you would like to know how to create one for your business, you might consider my book – *Professional Online Newsletters and Emails – Exactly how to create your own*. View it on www.successis.co.nz/books.htm)

Plain text only?

Make sure your plain text email has your good string of words before any design elements such as lines, symbols or hyperlinks.

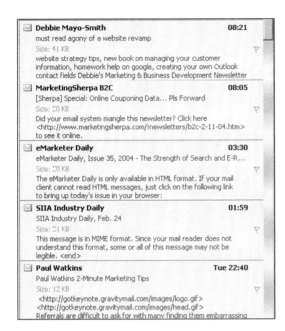

Figure 7 *See how my preview compares with other newsletters?*

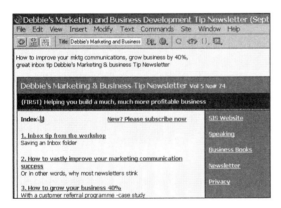

Figure 8 *Type what you want to be previewed. Control your preview destiny!*

CHAPTER THIRTEEN

Help!
How can I make email
marketing easier?

Solutions in this chapter

☑ Automatic responses

☑ Automating information to go directly from web to database

☑ Clever techniques for automatic sorting and handling

Are you experiencing any of these problems?

1. I spend too much time reading and responding to my incoming email marketing responses.

2. I spend too much time manually typing new subscriber details into my mailing list.

3. I get lots of emails originating from different parts of my website, and it's cumbersome handling them all.

Boy, do I have solutions for you!

Secrets

It would be remiss of me not to share some of my email marketing secrets with you in this book. We've been using email successfully for many years now. In fact, it's the only way we physically market our products and services – through email to our own private list of subscribers, plus clever Internet marketing joint ventures and strategies. And I'm not sure if 'physically' is the right word.

Business strength

One of our strengths has always been our ability to cope with a lot of administrative work, handled by very few people. The secret to this success is that from day one I decided to **automate**. Let the computers, the software do the work whereever possible instead of us manually doing it.

5-Step Plan: how to eliminate 98% of your manual admin work

Here's the general strategy we follow. As you read through it, adapt it for your business.

1. We centre as much data entry as possible on the website. This includes new subscriptions to our newsletter, orders, registrations, queries from the website and requests for quotes for our different services or products.

2. All this information (that the client keys in) goes into online databases **AND** comes to us as an email telling us the event has occurred (newsletter subscription, order, registration, unsubscribe, etc.).

3. We use Outlook Rules. All the incoming emails either have unique email addresses or the subject line is pre-coded so they can all be automatically sorted upon arrival in our Inbox.

4. We download the online databases, cut the information and paste it into our master databases held in the computer (newsletter mailing list, book sales, workshop registration, etc.). This is instead of having to manually type each one in. We delete the information we took from the online database and put it back online. Fresh, clean and empty.

5. We designed several Word document templates with built-in 'if statements' that read the data. It's miraculous – with one push

of a button Word will automatically produce all the correct receipts and invoices – New Zealand, Australia and Rest of the World (GST or plain and all kinds of permutations) in one single go.

SO HOW DO I DO ALL THIS?

By far the most important concept for you is to move information capture to 'website to database' instead of only 'website to email'.

You would not believe how easy and inexpensive it is to have your website enquiries and transactions being recorded in a database instead of coming in as just an email (and you manually adding it into your database). You absolutely should demand this from your website designer if you haven't done so already.

Web to database instead of web to email – background knowledge

Many people will just have on their websites 'Sign up for our newsletter by clicking here'. The link creates an email addressed to them/the company. Once clicked by the viewer, an email opens in their email program, and they probably will just hit Send.

That's not a lot of help to you, for two reasons

First, unless they have an automatic signature (see Chapter Seven), all you have to put in your database is their email address. And take it from me – if you're ever going to want to market to your database, it's much better to have information about them so you can target. Get their name and where they live at least!

Second, it will only come to you in an email. So you have to copy the information and then open up your database and paste it in.

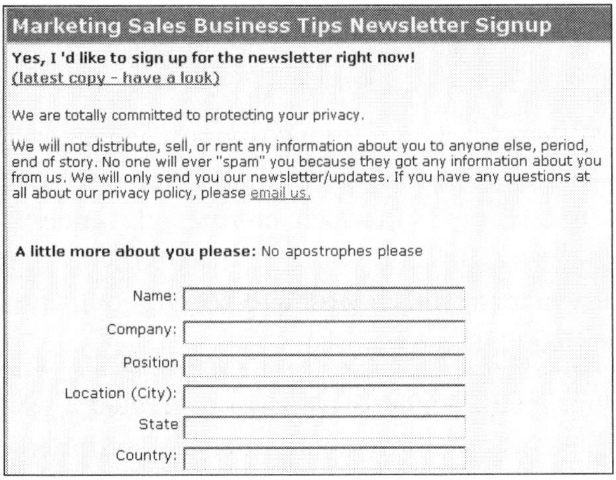

Figure 1 *This is part of our newsletter sign-up form on the website. This is how the page looks on the Internet in Internet Explorer.*

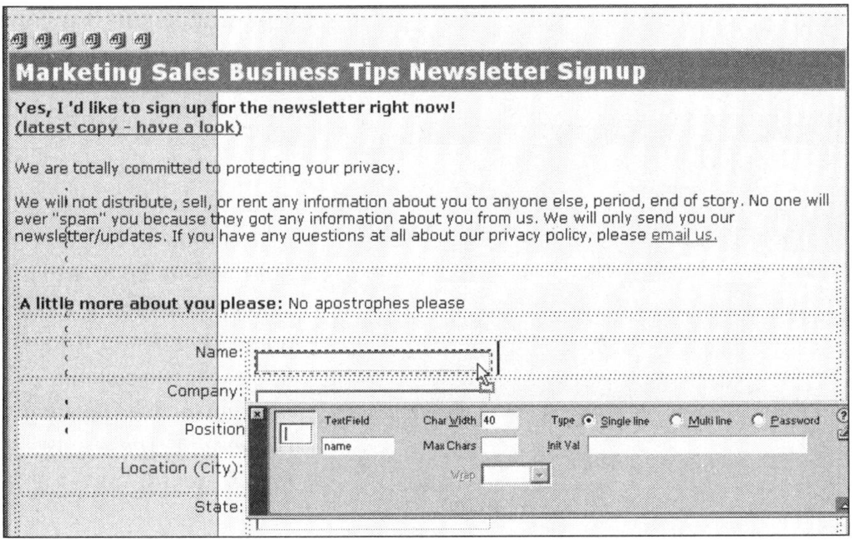

Figure 2 *This is how the same information looks in Macromedia Dreamweaver (our web design software).*

What a lot of work this is over time, wouldn't you agree?

Forms to collect data

When anything other than a 'click here' email response is required, you have to create a **form**. A form is placed on a web page and contains fill-in blanks, or form fields, in which information is entered. The form needs to be given directions on what to do with that information, including where to send it. Most web hosting companies have standard form coding that can be used.

Most likely you or your web designer have already created a web page with a form in it to collect information. Orders, subscriptions, changes of address, queries, etc. But the information might be just coming to you in an email. If this is what is happening, again it means needless manual work for you.

Instead, have a database created to accumulate and store the

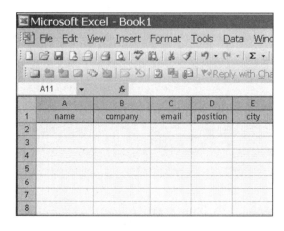

Figure 3 *Each piece of information on the form has to be matched with a column in a database. So, name from the form goes into the name column, position into the position column, etc. These must match exactly.*

information. This database can be an Excel spreadsheet, an Access Table, ACT, or any other database program you're using.

A bit more technical information

Look at Figure 4. This is my newsletter sign-up form, a few questions down from those illustrated in Figures 1 and 2. The view is from Macromedia Dreamweaver web-design software.

The menu bar to the right in Figure 4 is for creating forms. It has different options available, such as radio buttons, check boxes, and text fields. You chose which to use based on the information you want to collect. A check box means a yes or no answer. A text box is where you collect written information like name, position, city. Radio buttons can be used when you have several different possible answers for one question.

The menu bar on the bottom of Figure 4 shows you the specifics of each form item you create. I've used radio buttons for my format question '**I'd prefer the newsletter in this format.**'

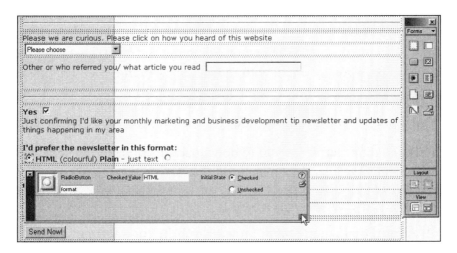

Figure 4 *Each field on the form has to be named. This name must match* **exactly** *the column name you have in your database. In this example, I have called the form field 'format'. If I had 'newsletter format' as a column heading in the database, it wouldn't work. The two radio button choices (HTML or plain text) are both named 'format', but they differ in their checked value. If you didn't have the checked value named, how would you know what the person had selected?*

Top Tip

If you have one or three – or even seven – possible choices for an answer in one database column, always be sure to give them the same field name (my example = format). Give each radio button different Checked Value names so you'll know what has been selected.

So far we have mentioned:

- You need a **form** to gather information.

- You need an **online database** for the information to feed into.

There's one crucial ingredient missing.

The third requirement – instructions!

The instructions are a two-fold process. First, the form needs to be given a function. To be activated. There has to be code to tell the form (once someone has clicked that Submit/Send button) to 'look for a page of code that tells you exactly what to do with the data'. Where to find the correct database. Where to put the information in. To say thank you to the person filling out the form. Last, but not least, to send you an email with the information in it too. That page of code is the second part of the process.

You'll need to have your web designer do this for you.

Then, all that's left is for you to download the information collected online and add it to your master database.

In summary, what you need is:

1. A form that people fill in on your website (or a form in an email you send out).

2. A web designer to write code for the back of the form to activate it. There are normally five to eight lines of code. Figure 5 shows the back of our signup form.

3. A web designer to write the rest of the code. A web page with code (JavaScript, PHP, ASP, DHTML, etc.) telling the form where to look for the database and how to match the information from the form to the database.

4. A database hosted on your website. Don't forget that the form fields and the database column names must match exactly.

5. Access to your website FTP (file transfer protocol), so you can download the online databases with the information they've accumulated into your computer.

```
<form method="post" action="http://www.successis.co.nz/asp/rw123form.asp"
name="Website newsletter subscription">
  <input type="hidden" name="mailto" value="subscribeSIS@successis.co.nz">
  <input type="hidden" name="subject" value="SIS Website newsletter subscription">
  <input type="hidden" name="mailfrom" value="site@successis.co.nz">
  <input type="hidden" name="thankurl" value="http://www.successis.co.nz/thanks/thanks.htm">
  <input type="hidden" name="inputform" value="newsletter/sign-up.htm">
  <input type="hidden" name="tablename" value="Subscribed">
```

Figure 5 *This is the form coding from the back of my newsletter sign-up web page. This is what kicks it into action!*

CAN I USE THIS FOR EMAIL SURVEYS?

Surveys are simply forms that you email. It doesn't matter if someone is filling in just an email address or a 15-question survey. By having responses go to a database, doing an online survey can be effortless – and you eliminate 95% of the work. No more manual entering or cutting/pasting from emails. Only from the people that have faxed you back!

One caveat: I find not all systems handle forms perfectly. For someone to respond to an emailed form, they have to have Internet access. Not all employees have that. They could have email – but not an Internet connection to their computer. Also, the email has to be clicked open rather than answered in the Preview/Reading Pane.

What about all those emails coming in, Debbie?

Here's where the magic of Rules and clever thinking really comes into play.

We've spoken about Rules throughout this book. Hopefully you are familiar with them by now, and will have thought how you can set up Rules to handle your incoming web order emails, requests for information from your email marketing, and so on.

Now, here are two utterly fabulous tips to make it **so much easier** to set up Rules. You can pre-code the subject line of emails coming in to you, and also create fake email addresses. By precoding I mean when the recipient clicks on your email link the subject line is automatically filled out.

Pre-code subject line of Email

Pre-coding your Subject line manually

Simply add right after the end of your **mail to** address: **?subject=and_what_you_want** (after the .co.nz/.com.zu/.com, etc.)

No spaces. Add an underscore between words (so the sentence doesn't break). For example:

mailto:debbie@successis.co.nz?subject=more_information_on_ books_please

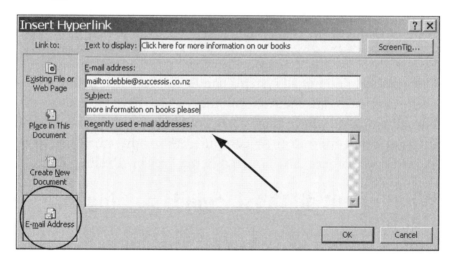

Figure 6 *Controlling how the subject line of a reply email coming in to you reads.*

Pre-coding in a Word Document (Figure 6)

1. Open the **hyperlink dialogue box** by one of these three methods:

    a. Highlight the text you want hyperlinked and hit ctrl+k or

    b. Highlight the text and click the hyperlink icon (a blue-green circle with a chain under it) or

    c. Highlight the text, go to the **Insert** menu, select **Hyperlink**.

2. In the dialogue box, select **Email address** in the bottom left-hand corner.

3. Type in whatever you desire.

Pre-coding the body of an email

You can manually precode the body of an email too.

Simply add **&body=** at the end of your subject line pre-coding (no spaces) and type the text you desire in the same way.

Fake email addresses

Normally, for domain email administration one email account (typically the administrator) is designated to receive any email addresses that do not exist for that domain. For example, misspelt names, ex-employees, etc.

You can take advantage of this by having your computer designated to receive these non-existent email addresses. Create any and all email addresses you want, and use them for your email and website response management. For example: if I am running a workshop in Melbourne, I'll have registrations come to registermelb@successis. co.nz instead of my debbie@successis.co.nz. And of course I'll have a Rule set up to put those emails in my Melbourne Registration folder!

Examples:

subscribe@yourcompany
unsubscribe@yourcompany
contest@yourcompany
survey@yourcompany

product1@yourcompany

product2@yourcompany

How do I automate handling all these requests coming in?

Autoresponses

Chapter Nine detailed how you can create an automatic response for being away from home or the office by creating an email template, and then setting up a Rule to send it.

You can also create a Rule to send an automatic pre-written response to any of your incoming emails, of course.

For example, do you get a lot of enquiries for information on this or that product or service from your website? Instead of individually responding to each and every new one over and over again rewriting the same thing – set up an **Autoresponse**.

HOW DO I SET UP AN AUTORESPONSE?

1. Write a great email.

2. Save it as a template.

3. On your website, where you have 'click here for us to send you more information', either pre-code the subject line or use a special email address.

4. Create a Rule that looks for that incoming email, sends a response, and puts the email in a folder.

5. Check the new emails in the folder every day or two. You'll have automatically responded to the enquiries, but you wouldn't have seen if the originator had typed in any other questions that need answering.

Top Tip

Automate movement of incoming email campaign responses straight into the correct folders – see Chapter One.

HOW DO I CREATE THOSE WORD DOCUMENTS WITH THE BUILT-IN 'IF' STATEMENTS?

You'll find the IF field in **Word Mail Merge** (Tools > Letters and Mailing > Mail Merge). On the **Mail Merge** toolbar, select **Insert Word Field** and then click **IF . . . Then . . . Else**.

IF performs one of two actions, depending on the condition you set. For example, if the form contains NZ or AUS, put in GST; if it doesn't (have the words NZ or AUS), don't put in GST.

The condition specified is whether the words NZ or AUS were found. If this condition is met, a certain action takes place (putting GST in the document). If the condition is not met, an alternative action occurs (leaving the GST out).

You can also nest the statements. In other words: If a merge field has 'X' put this content. If the merge field has 'Y' put this content. If the merge field has 'Z' put this content.

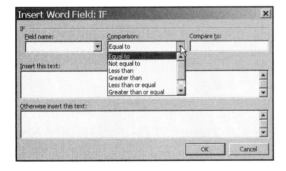

Figure 7 *The* **IF . . . Then . . . Else** *dialogue box.*

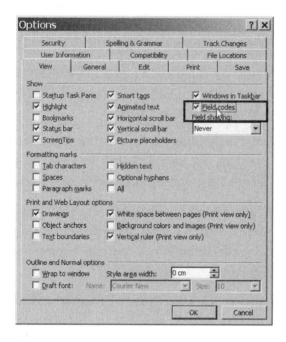

Figure 8 *When you select field codes you'll see all the hidden fields. You'll be able to apply formatting to your IF statements by checking this box. When you're through, un-select it (you'll know what I mean by this if you ever use this function).*

As you can imagine, if you dissect the variables in your invoices/receipts/letters/emails you'll be able to do things you've never imagined before – just by learning that hidden merge field jewel **IF . . . Then . . . Else.**

Formatting that IF Text

We've going ultra-techie here. Did you want to apply formatting to the results of your hidden **IF . . . Then . . . Else** statements? You probably wonder how on earth you can, since they're hidden! Well, here's where having a Chief Information Officer for a husband helped me, as I would never in a million years have found this.

In Microsoft®Word, on the **Tool** menu, under **Options**, select the check box for **Field Codes** (as shown in Figure 8). Or as Kirsty (my right hand) found: ALT+F9.

CHAPTER FOURTEEN

Help!
How can I keep on top of projects, quotes and who's doing what?

> **Solutions in this chapter**
>
> ☑ Put **Tasks** to work for you

Putting Tasks to work

I mentioned in Chapter Five that Tasks is one of my favourite tools in Outlook. There, you learnt how to create a Task from the perspective of an automatic To Do list. Tasks is great to prompt you to follow up on quotes, proposals, calls to make or important emails that you haven't heard back from.

However, Tasks has much more extensive uses.

HOW CAN I USE TASKS?

- Manage projects.
- Create and assign a Task to a staff member.
- Remind yourself to follow up on an email that came in.
- Remind yourself to check if you haven't received a response to an important email, call or document you sent.
- Track a project through from start to finish.
- Create a recurring Task.

- Assign time, work, mileage and billing information to a Task.
- Track staff follow-through.

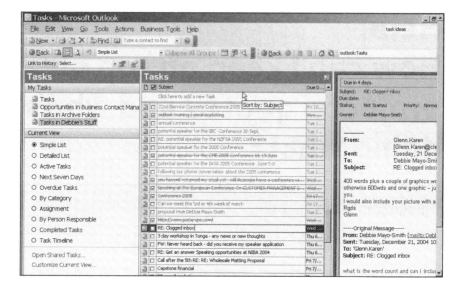

Figure 1 *Tasks viewed as a simple list. You can tell how diligent you've been. Overdue Tasks turn red. Ones that are current or haven't come up yet are in black, and completed tasks are grey with a line through them.*

Top Tip

Animated Microsoft Online Tutorial on Tasks:

http://office.microsoft.com/en-au/assistance/
HA010929451033.aspx

WHAT CAN I DO WITH MY TASKS?

Task tab

On each Task you can:

1. Set who the Task belongs to.
2. Assign it to someone.
3. Make it recurring.
4. Assign a due date.

5. Assign a start date.

6. Assign and change its status (not started, in progress, etc.).

7. Give it a priority.

8. Assign a percentage complete.

9. Set a reminder, and set that date and time.

10. Assign contacts to it.

11. Assign categories to it.

12. Make it a private Task.

Moving on to the Details tab

You can also:

13. Assign a date completed.

14. Assign the Total Work Hours.

15. Assign the Actual Work Hours.

16. Assign mileage.

17. Assign billing information.

Top Tip

When I send important email, I Bcc myself (blind carbon copy). When my copy arrives, I drag & drop it into Tasks.

A brand new task opens, with the content of my email in its text field. I then give it a subject, due date and save it. I then delete that email to me in my Inbox (it's not necessary any more, the content is in the Task). When I'm reminded on the due date, I move the Task to an email (File > Move or Copy), delete all the 'Task' stuff in this new email, and type in my new message.

HOW DO I CREATE A TASK?

On the **File** menu, point to **New**, and then click **Task**.

HOW DO I MAKE THE TASK RECUR?

To make the task recur, click **Recurrence,** and click the frequency (**Daily, Weekly, Monthly, Yearly**) at which you want the task to recur. Then do one of the following:

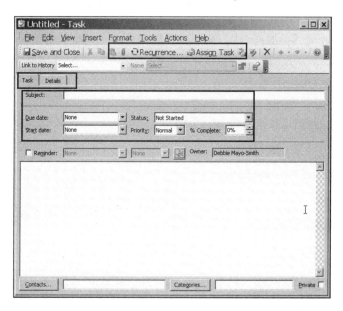

Figure 2 *A blank Task. Note all the settings you can use.*

Make the Task recur at regular intervals

1. Select the options you want for that frequency.

2. Do not click **Regenerate new task,** or the task will not recur at regular intervals.

3. Click **OK,** and then click **Save and Close**.

Make the Task recur based on completion date

1. Click **Regenerate new task,** and then type a time frequency in the box. If you want, set start and end dates for the task.

2. Click **OK,** and then click **Save and Close**.

HOW DO I CREATE A TASK FROM AN EXISTING TASK?

1. In Task list, select the task you want to copy.

2. On the **Edit** menu, click **Copy**. If the **Copy** command is not available, click the check mark in the Task's **Icon** column, and then try again.

3. On the **Edit** menu, click **Paste**.

4. As appropriate, open the Task and change its options.

5 more great Task tips
How do I . . .

1. QUICKLY MARK A TASK AS COMPLETE?

Right-click the Task and then click **Mark Complete** on the shortcut menu.

2. QUICKLY ASSIGN A TASK?

Right-click the Task, and then on the shortcut menu, click **Assign Task** and type a name in the **To** box.

3. CHANGE THE ORDER OF TASKS IN A TASK LIST?

In the **Task** pane, when Tasks aren't grouped or sorted, just drag the Tasks up or down in the task list.

4. QUICKLY CREATE A TASK FROM A FILE CONTAINING DETAILS ABOUT THE TASK?

Drag the file to the **Tasks** button and drop it. A new Task opens with the file attached. Fill in the rest of the information about the Task, and then click **Save and Close**.

5. QUICKLY SEND A NEW EMAIL ABOUT A TASK?

Drag the Task to the **Mail** button and drop it. This creates a new email with the Task name as the subject and the Task details in the body of the email.

GET MUCH MUCH MORE OUT OF OUTLOOK

CHAPTER FIFTEEN

Help!
How can I make my
Contacts more useful
(personal and business)?

Solutions in this chapter

☑ Compare what you can store in Outlook and Outlook Express

☑ The little known secret of **Categories** revealed

☑ Using **Organize** to sort out lots of Contacts

Outlook *vs* Outlook Express Contacts

Both Outlook and Outlook Express call the 'home' of your contacts **Address Book**. The individual people that populate your address book(s) are called Contacts.

The information can be simple (just a name and email address) or much more detailed – such as all their business and personal contact information, company information and web address.

The fields of information that both Outlook and Outlook Express carry are very similar, although Outlook is more comprehensive. Compare Figure 2 (Outlook Express) with Figure 3 (Outlook).

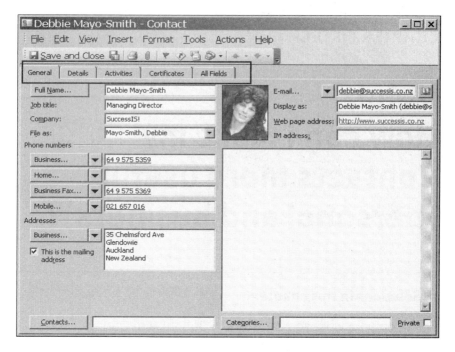

Figure 1 *The contact information you can store in Outlook. The newer versions allow you to add photos of your contacts.*

> **Top Tip**
>
> I did a keynote presentation at the Barfoot and Thompson Real Estate National Conference. One of the subjects of the speech was the importance of keeping a good database.
>
> One very clever lady wrote to me that she was using Contacts to store her property information – and she put the picture of the house in the contact photo field.

Why store detailed information in Contacts?

If you are using Outlook or Outlook Express for personal use only, you wouldn't need detailed business information – but you might want to keep information such as spouse and children names, as in Figure 4.

But for business, you would need such information. Why?
Let me just give you an excerpt from my book *Superb Tip and Tricks For Managing Your Customer Information* (www.successis.co.nz/books.htm).

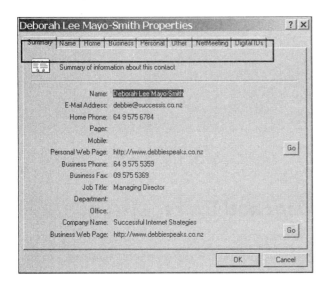

Figure 2 *Outlook Express carries similar information to Outlook. The information is keyed in on different tabs.*

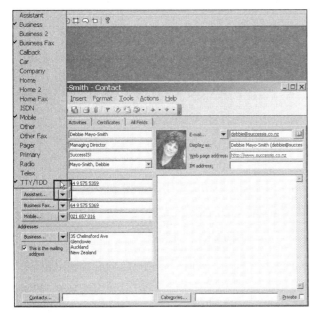

Figure 3 *There's much more than meets the eye in Outlook Contacts. Click on any of the drop-down menus, and you'd be amazed at the variety of information you can store.*

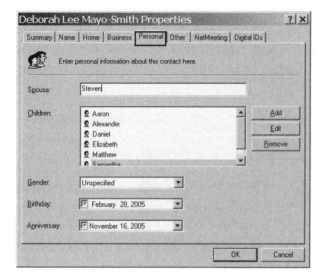

Figure 4 *Outlook Express 6 gives you the ability to store children's as well as spouse names for your contacts.*

From *Superb Tips and Tricks* (page 9)

To be effective in marketing today, be it online or in print communications to your customers and prospects, you need to be targeted.

Pertinent and valuable

People are overloaded with information. If what they receive is not pertinent, or adds value to them, then they won't read it! Very quickly you'll also lose your permission to correspond or to use email with them.

To add value, to target, you cannot treat everyone the same. You wouldn't want to try to sell meat to a vegetarian would you? To treat people and businesses differently, you need accurate information about them.

Valuable customer knowledge lost

But what if that information is in your head? Or in the head of your employees? Or on a piece of paper? You can't move with speed. You can't contact many clients at a time. You can lose valuable customer knowledge if an employee leaves.

So you've got to take all the information from your head, from your employee's heads, from paper files and merge it in **one** place in the computer. Build a marketing database or enhance the one you have.

Why have a centralised source of information? The reason is fourfold.

Personalised communications with a push of a button

First, when you have all that customer and prospective customer information in one spot in your computer you can literally (with the push of a button) create terrific marketing, business development, customer service and communication letters and emails – all personalised with any piece of information in your database. This will significantly help you to build a much, much more profitable business. How? By simultaneously helping to lower your marketing and operating costs and bring in new business and income. With ease.

Increase your business value

Second, a good marketing database can help increase the value of your business when you go to sell it. It makes a much more valuable going concern.

Someone else does the work

Third, when the information is in the database, any assistant can create marketing campaigns, customer prompts, monthly newsletters and send them without you doing the manual work. It can't get better than that.

Everyday software is marvellous

Fourth, you would not believe how easy it is to do all this just using the everyday software you have. There are so many features you probably don't know about that will save you literally hours and hours and hours of time. I'll tell you all of them.

Categories

Hopefully, that excerpt helped you to understand the value of keeping and storing information, and thus your ability to **target**.

Let me introduce you to one of the best kept secrets and most under-utilised assets in Outlook Contacts. And that's **Categories**.

Note: Categories are not available in Outlook Express.

What are categories?

A category is a keyword or key phrase that you can assign to a contact. Or an email. Or an appointment. Or a Task! You can assign one or as many categories as you like to each item. We'll focus on contacts in this chapter.

Why are categories so utterly brilliant?

Four reasons:

1. They help you to categorise and target your contacts by what is important to you (or, more wisely, to them). You can create, for example, categories by industry, by company size, by their nature of business with you.

2. They're great for organisation. By assigning categories to contacts (or emails, or tasks) you can easily find, sort, filter, or group them by category.

3. Use Categories to keep track of different types of items that are related but stored in different folders. For example, you can keep track of all the meetings, contacts, and emails for a baseball committee you're on, or any business project. Create a category (**Baseball** or **New Project**), and assign items to it.

4. Categories also give you a way to keep track of items without putting them in separate folders. For example, you can keep business and personal tasks in the same **Task list** and use the **Business** and **Personal** categories to view the tasks separately.

Top Tip
Categories are not just for contacts!

You can assign categories to emails, appointments, tasks, journal entries, notes, posted items and documents.

The Master Category List

Microsoft® Outlook supplies a list of categories, called the **Master Category List**. You can use this list as it is, or add your own categories to it.

Based on how you like to work, you can:

- Create new categories in the Master Category List **in advance** and then assign contacts to them later.

- Assign items one at a time to categories **as you create each item**.

Remember: a contact can be assigned to more than one category. For example, it can be classified as a Key Customer, Small Business Owner, (your) Newsletter Recipient . . .

Top Tip
STOP! Think very carefully.

Take a walk; take time out. Think about your business and what you want to accomplish with categorising. What are your communication goals? Next, plan what information you need to do it well. *Then* start setting up your categories and getting the information.

HOW DO I CREATE A NEW CATEGORY?

1. Select any contact (or email, task, or calendar item for that matter).

2. On the **Edit** menu, click **Categories**.

3. Click **Master Category List**.

4. In the **New category** box, type a name for the category.

5. Click **Add**.

6. To create more categories, repeat steps 4 and 5.

7. Click **OK** twice.

Figure 5 *It's easy to create a new category. To get to the Master Category List: when you have a contact open (if you don't then the Categories will be greyed out), select Categories from the Edit menu. Then select the Master Category List button.*

Figure 6 *When creating a new category, please don't just type it into the box. Select the Master Category List first, then type.*

Top Tip

How do I assign a category when creating a contact?

Just click the **Categories** button in the bottom right corner.

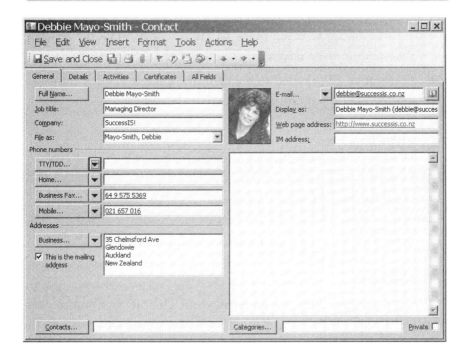

Figure 7 *The* **Categories** *button is in the bottom centre of every contact you create.*

Top Tip

Tasks also has a Category tab on each task. However, for assigning a category to an email, you first click **Options**, and then click **Categories**.

HOW DO I ASSIGN A CATEGORY TO AN EXISTING CONTACT (OR OTHER ITEM)?

1. Select the item you want to assign to a category.

2. On the **Edit** menu, click **Categories**.

3. In the **Available categories** list, select the check boxes next to the categories you want, and then click **OK**.

If a check box is shaded, some of the items selected in step 1 are already assigned to that category.

- To add all the selected items to the category, click the shaded check box until a check mark without shading appears.

- To remove all selected items from the category, click the shaded check box until it is clear.

Top Tip

By using categories with your contacts, you can keep them all in one Contact folder instead of the old way of creating multiple Contact groups based on categories. This way, you can sort one large group by categories when you need to send an email to a group of contacts.

Too late!?

Are you thinking, 'This is wonderful stuff, Debbie, but you're years too late! I've got hundreds or thousands of contacts and this is in the too hard basket.'?

Well, I've got a wonderful quick solution for you. It's called **Organize** and you'll find it in the **Tools** menu.

Once you have Organize open you can categorise your contacts en masse!

Top Tip

May I suggest you have a play with how you view your contacts first?

This concept of changing views is discussed in more detail in Chapter Twenty-one. If you view your contacts by location or by company, you'll be able to get a much larger list from which to select.

HOW DO I APPLY CATEGORIES TO LOTS OF CONTACTS AT ONCE?

1. Select **Tools, Organize**.

2. There are two ways to select groups of contacts.

    a. **To select a whole chunk of contacts:**

    Click on the first Contact you want to categorise. Then scroll down to the last one. Hold down the SHIFT key and then click. This will select all of the ones between the first and the one selected.

    b. **To select contacts as you scroll down your list, skipping ones here and there:**

    Click on your first one, then hold down the CTRL key and select the contacts you want to categorise.

3. With your selections made, in the **Using Categories** section of Organize either click the drop-down box under **Add contacts selected below** to or type in a new category under the **Create a new category** window.

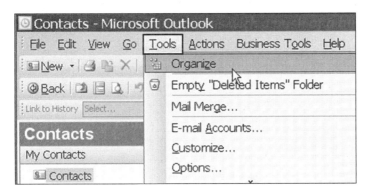

Figure 8 *To start a mass categorisation of your contacts, I suggest you go to Tools > Organize.*

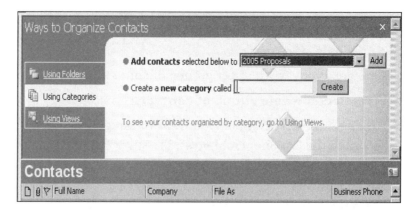

Figure 9 *Using Organize, under your Tools menu, allows you to assign categories to many contacts at once.*

Top Tip

Be sure when creating a new category you don't just type it in (as in Figure 6).

It has to be entered into the Master Category List for it to be recognised for sorting and working with in the future.

CHAPTER SIXTEEN

Help!
How can I use Contacts for my marketing?

Solutions in this chapter

☑ How to **Mail Merge** from Contacts

Mail Merging from Contacts

'Oh my Goodness!' I said.

'I can't believe it. Do you know how much time, energy and money this has just saved us?' That was Kirsty, my right hand at the office.

What we were gleefully talking about was our first use of the Microsoft® Office email merge. We had just sent over 100 personalised, colourful and formatted emails to overseas clients. Since then we have used it scores of times. But then again, one of the foundations of my business is regular communication (with anyone that wants to be educated and hear from us).

Normally, marketing and customer relationship management is hard. It can be expensive. It's the one part of your business that's easy to put off. However, you can be the best in your field – but if no one knows about you, what good is that?

Why not create a strategic competitive advantage for your business and free up one of your most precious commodities – time?

Devise a clever and 'what's in it for them?' communication strategy for your clients and prospective clients. Consider using email as the communication vehicle, rather than the post. And the best thing about this? You'll be able to do so much more, at practically no cost.

You've got the tools at your fingertips with Contacts and Mail Merge.

What is a mail merge?

A mail merge is a procedure in which you take your Contact information and merge it into individual mailing labels, envelopes, emails, invoices, receipts, form letters, catalogues or faxes.

Outlook

You can begin a mail/email merge straight from Outlook or from Microsoft® Word using your Contact information (or any database for the merge!).

Outlook Express

A big difference between Outlook and Outlook Express is that Microsoft® automatically integrates information between Outlook and the other Office programs. It doesn't with Outlook Express. So while you can directly do a mail merge from your Outlook Contacts, you can't do a mail/email merge from Outlook Express.

BUT WAIT!

Before you get all bummed out, I didn't say you *couldn't* do a mail merge with your Outlook Express Contact information. You can get around it by exporting your Outlook Express Contact details to Excel, and then conducting the mail/email merge straight from Microsoft® Word.

Top Tip
Merging is not just with Contacts, and not just from Outlook!

You can merge any piece of information you have from any database into a letter or email. This is significant as it gives you a tremendous opportunity to customise, personalise, automate and create merges you never thought possible, with a little forethought and creativity. Invoices, receipts, invitations personalised by city and venue instead of blanket ones listing all the cities, times and venues. The limit is your imagination.

HOW DO I CHOOSE WHICH CONTACTS TO MERGE?

You can choose which contacts will be part of the mail merge in five ways:

1. Select *all* your contacts.
2. Select specific contacts from the **Contacts** folder by clicking them while holding down the CTRL key.
3. Create a separate contacts folder and copy only the contacts you need to that folder.
4. View contacts by category and select the category.
5. Create a custom view of the **Contacts** folder. For example, you can create a view that contains only your contacts from a particular state/province and then send an email to them only.

WHAT CONTACT FIELDS CAN I INCLUDE?

You might not realise it, but there are almost 100 fields available for each Outlook Contact (see page 206)! Most aren't used, and only a small fraction are listed in your Contacts folder when you view your contacts.

Once you decide which contacts you want merged, you can further specify which fields to include. For example, you might want **First Name, Last Name, Street Address,** and **Postal Code,** but not **Country** or **Phone**. Or you might want to do an email merge and you just require **First Name** and **Email Address. You can only merge the fields that are showing on your screen.**

YOU'VE GOT TO SEE IT TO MERGE IT

If a field isn't showing in your **Contact View,** you can add it with **Field Chooser**.

1. Right-click the top grey bar containing the field names (in Figure 1 you see the field names of **Full Name** and **Email**).

2. Select **Field Chooser** from the list.

3. Next select what field list you want to view (name, email, etc.) and it will show the fields available.

4. Finally, just grab the field you want, drag it to the column headers and drop it where you want it located (our old friend drag & drop again.)

When you start a mail merge from Outlook, the contacts you select are exported to a temporary mail merge source file, to a printer, or to an email, depending on what option you choose. You can save the temporary mail merge source file if you want to use the same contacts for future mail merges.

Distribution lists (Groups) cannot be included in a mail/email merge. You don't have to remove the personal distribution lists from Contacts, however. Outlook will ignore them. (I will show you in Chapter Seventeen how to get your individual email addresses out of a distribution list.)

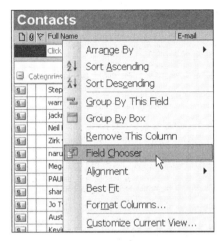

Figure 1 *To get a merge field that isn't showing in your current view, right-click the grey column headers and select Field Chooser.*

Figure 2 *Find the field you want from the selection of lists.*

Figure 3 *Drag & drop the field of your choice.*

Top Tip

Being a better marketer.

You know the old marketing concept of when you see articles or information that is of interest to your clients, you should send it to them?

Now, when you see an article or news item on the Internet that would be of interest to a certain category of client, you can copy it and paste it in an email or Word document (or just copy the hyperlink of the article).

Next sort your contacts by categories and do a personalised email merge to the whole category. Each one will receive an individual personalised email (especially if you use their first name as one of your merge fields).

They'll think you're wonderful just writing to them, when you could be doing this to 1001!

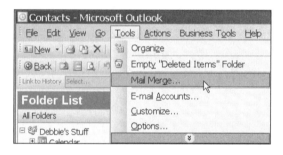

Figure 4 *A mail/email merge is stunningly simple with contacts. A Wizard walks you through it!*

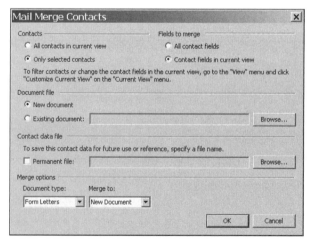

Figure 5 *The Mail Merge Contacts window.*

HOW DO I DO A MAIL MERGE FROM OUTLOOK CONTACTS?

1. On the **Tools** menu, click **Mail Merge**.

2. Under **Contacts**, click an option.

3. Under **Fields to merge**, click an option.

4. Under **Document file**, click an option.

   a. To add merge fields to a document you've already created, click **Existing document**, and then click **Browse** to select the document.

   b. To create a new document for the mail merge, click **New document**.

5. If you want to save the current set of contacts in a merge file, select the **Permanent file** check box, and then click **Browse** to select the document.

6. In the **Document type** list, select the type of mail merge you want.

7. In the **Merge to** list, select where you want the merged records exported to. Personal distribution lists are not exported.

8. Click **OK**. Microsoft® Word opens.

9. In Word, on the **Tools** menu, point to **Letters and Mailings**, and then click **Mail Merge Wizard** or use the **Mail Merge** toolbar.

10. Use Word **Help** for additional information.

Caveat: Outlook 2000 – the email merge is plain text only. (When you're doing the merge from Word, by the way, the selection to merge to email is the last step.)

In the 2002 and 2003 versions you have the choice of HTML formatting or plain text, and the email merge is one of the first options.

HOW DO I DO A MAIL MERGE FROM OUTLOOK EXPRESS CONTACTS?

1. On the **Tools** menu select **Export Address Book** (Chapter Seventeen walks you through this process). Save the file to Excel.

2. Open Word. On the **Tools** menu, point to **Letters and Mailings**, and then click **Mail Merge Wizard** or use the **Mail Merge** toolbar.

3. Use Word Help for additional information.

> **Top Tip**
> Microsoft tutorial on using the mail merge for mass mailings and more: http://office.microsoft.com/training/training.aspx?AssetID=RC 011205671033

8 more great Contact tips
How do I . . .

1. QUICKLY CREATE A CONTACT WITH THE SAME COMPANY NAME AND ADDRESS AS ANOTHER CONTACT?

Select the existing contact in your Contacts list. Then on the **Actions** menu, click **New Contact from Same Company**.

2. CREATE A TASK RELATED TO A CONTACT?

For example, invite to your next dinner party; call them in a month; send them a thank you note.
Click the contact, click the **Actions** menu, and then click **New Task for Contact**.

3. SET UP A SPEED-DIAL LIST?

On the **Actions** menu, point to **Call Contact**, click **New Call** and then click **Dialing Options**.

4. QUICKLY MOVE THROUGH CONTACT ADDRESS CARDS?

Use the arrow keys. Press HOME to move to the first card. Press END to move to the last card. Use the arrow keys to move up, down, and across the columns.

5. QUICKLY DIAL A PHONE NUMBER FOR A CONTACT?

This needs to be set up in your system first.
Right-click the contact, and then on the **shortcut** menu, click **Call Contact**.

6. SEND AN EMAIL QUICKLY TO A CONTACT?

Click the contact and then on the **Actions** menu, click **New Message to Contact**.

7. QUICKLY CHANGE THE NUMBER OF COLUMNS OF CONTACTS IN MY CONTACTS LIST?

This is when you have card or detailed card as your Contact view. Just drag one of the vertical dividers that separate the columns. Closer together shows more columns.

8. QUICKLY SCHEDULE A MEETING WITH A CONTACT?

Click the contact and then on the **Actions** menu, click **New Meeting Request to Contact**.

Keyboard Shortcuts for Contacts

ACTION	KEYBOARD SHORTCUT
Create a new contact	CTRL+SHIFT+C
Find a contact	F11
Save and close a contact	ALT+S
Delete a contact	CTRL+D

CHAPTER SEVENTEEN

Help!
What else can I do with
Contacts?

Solutions in this chapter

☑ Quickly create a new Contact

☑ Move your Contact information

☑ Customise the Contact form

A little jewel

First I must share with you what I think is a brilliant shortcut – one I found by a drag & drop accident.

Have an email from someone you'd like to add to your contacts? Perhaps you know that if you right-click the email address in the **From** column of that received email, an option is to add that person to your contacts. However, it will only put the name and email address into that new contact for you.

Here's the brilliant tip. If you drag that *entire* email and drop it into your Contacts folder, it will open a new Contact. The content of that email will be put in the Contact text box (See Figure 1), and the name and email address will populate the correct Contact fields. Now, that person may have further details in their email – most people do, with Signatures (Chapter Seven) – such as their address, phone number, position, web address. You can highlight each contact detail and drag and drop it into the appropriate Contact field. This little tip can save so much time typing things in manually. Try it – you'll love it!

You might be starting to realise by now that I have a thing about not doing things the long way!

Moving information in and out of Contacts

Contact problems?

Have you wanted to get information into or out of your contacts en masse?

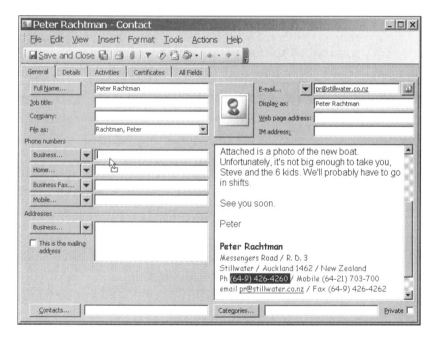

Figure 1 *Our friend Peter sent us an email about his new boat. But I didn't have his contact details. From the Inbox, I highlighted his email, dragged it over to my Contact folder and let go of the mouse. This new contact opened with Peter's name and email in the proper Contact fields and his message in the text box. I am going to highlight all his other contact details, and drag and drop them into their proper fields. You can see I've started with Stillwater Associates, which I'm in the process of dropping into the Company field.*

What if someone sends you an Excel spreadsheet or some other type of file with information that you would like to add into your Contacts?

What if you want to take your Outlook or Outlook Express contact information and move it to another database or program?

Need a clean? Too many useless contacts?

Your contacts might be a few years old by now. Surely you have some dead weight there, old information as well as many duplicates. I have many contacts where one person is listed three or four times because they have different email addresses or incomplete contact details.

Before the 2002 version of Outlook, you could automatically add anyone that you replied to into your Contacts (that functionality is gone now.) If you ever had that turned on, you might have an enormous list of contacts – with many that you don't know, recognise or need.

My advice

Export your contacts into Excel, clean them up there and then import them back into Contacts as a new Contact group. Make sure this new group is A-okay, then delete your old Contacts file.

SO HOW DO I MOVE INFORMATION?

There are three ways of moving information into and out of your contacts.

1. Copying and pasting.

2. Importing and exporting it.

3. Getting individual information out of a Group or Distribution list is a bit tricky but can be done. I'll show you how.

Copy and paste is too easy to write about

One of the utter pleasures of working within Microsoft® software is how easy it is to copy anything from one program and paste it into any of the others. If you wanted to copy your contacts from the screen (remember it will only copy what it sees – the fields showing), you can paste them into an Access table, into Excel or into Word (they'll create their own table).

For example, let's say you sort your Contacts by a category and want to move that to an Excel spreadsheet. It's as simple as this:

Full Name	Company	E-mail	Bu...	Categories
Click here to add a new C...				
Debbie Tawse	Celebrity Speake...	info@...	+6...	Speaker Bureau
David Maher	Celebrity Speakers	daivd...		Speaker Bureau
Carson White	ICMI	carso...	(0...	Speaker Bureau
Graham Anderson	Saxton	gande...		Speaker Bureau
Peter Physick	ICMI Castle Hill	peter...	+6...	Speaker Bureau
Julie Anchors	EnterTainers an...	julie@...	61...	Speaker Bureau
Margaret Booth	Great Expectatio...	marga...	+6...	Speaker Bureau
David Maher	Celebrity Speakers	david...	61...	Speaker Bureau
Michelle Lee Brown	Celebrity Speake...	michell...	+6...	Speaker Bureau
Jane Pavlovic	Great Expectation	jane@...		Speaker Bureau
Leonie Scott	Great Expectation	leonie...		Speaker Bureau

Figure 2 *Copy and paste is as easy as selecting the contacts you want (here I've selected my Speakers' Bureau category) and pasting them into a blank Excel spreadsheet.*

highlight the information; select **Copy** and then open up Excel and hit **Paste**!

OUTLOOK: HOW DO I TAKE INFORMATION IN OR OUT OF CONTACTS?

Open Outlook, and go into your Contacts folder. We'll cover exporting here. Importing is just the opposite.

1. Under **File**, select **Import and Export**. (In Outlook 2003 you must select **Outlook** or **Business Contact Manager**.) A simple Wizard follows (Figure 3).

2. Select that you want to export to a file (Figure 4).

3. The file type should be **Excel** (Figure 5).

4. Confirm that it is the folder **Contacts** that you are exporting (Figure 6).

5. Browse to select where you want the file to be stored (Figure 7).

6. **Hit Finish**. Voilà . . . you have the start of your database, or all your contact information at your fingertips (Figure 8).

Top Tip

When importing information into Contacts, use the **Map Fields** step to match your database fields to those in Outlook.

You might have the name Phone in your database, whereas Outlook calls it Business Phone. So you need to tell Outlook – when you import this information, put Phone into the Business Phone column (Figure 9).

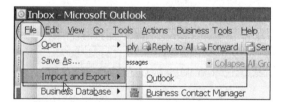

Figure 3 *Step one – in Contacts, File > Import and Export.*

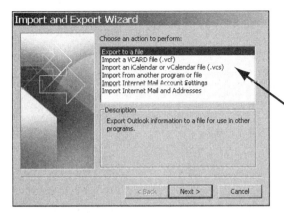

Figure 4 *Step two – you're asked to choose an action to perform (Export or Import). Select Export to a file.*

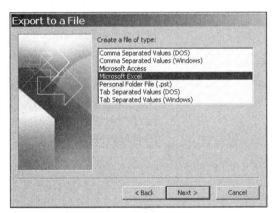

Figure 5 *Step three – select Microsoft Excel as the type of file to be created. Or Access if you like. If you're taking it into another make of software, like ACT, FileMakerPro, etc., select a CSV file [Comma Separated Values (DOS)] or a TAB file [Tab Separated Values (Windows)]. These are the common database languages.*

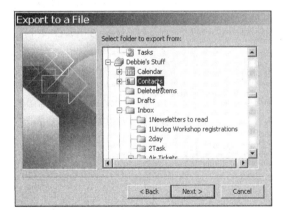

Figure 6 *Step four – select where you want to export from.*

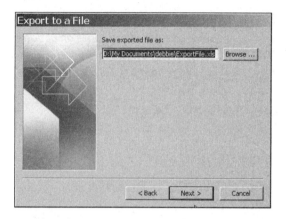

Figure 7 *Step five – where do you want this new file to be saved?*

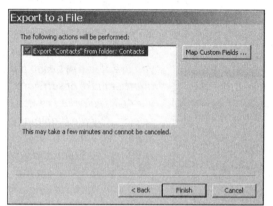

Figure 8 *Step six – now is when you click Finish. If you have a large amount of contacts, the process can take a few minutes and can't be interrupted. You might need to Map Custom Fields first – see Figure 9.*

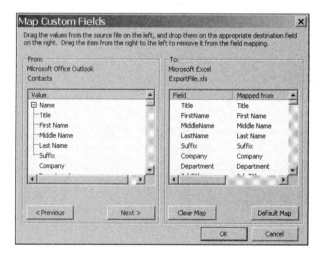

Figure 9 *Optional step: Mayo Custom Fields – when importing data into Contacts, use this to match your existing column headings to the ones already named in Contacts. You might have a field called Business, where Contacts calls it Company.*

OUTLOOK EXPRESS ADDRESS BOOK: HOW DO I EXPORT TO EXCEL?

Exporting from Outlook Express is very similar to exporting from Outlook.

1. With your Address Book open in Outlook Express, Select **File > Export > Other Address Book** (Figure 10).

2. Select a **Text File CSV** (Figure 11).

3. Select where you would like the file stored (Figure 12).

4. Check (select) which fields you want to have exported (Figure 13).

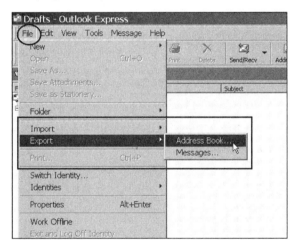

Figure 10 *Step one – with your Address Book open in Outlook Express, Select File > Export > Other Address Book.*

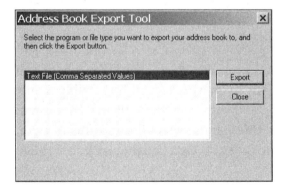

Figure 11 *Step two – export the address book to a CSV file.*

Figure 12
*Step three –
select where
you want the
new file to be
stored. Name
it.*

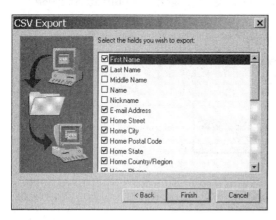

Figure 13 *Step four –
select what fields you'd like
to include in your new file.*

There you go. Your start to a new database.

WHERE'S MY FILE GONE?

Want your new file? Open Excel and go to the folder where you stored it. Now, don't freak out – you won't see it! It probably is only showing you Excel files now, and your new file is still in CSV format. At the bottom of the **Open File** menu, where it says **Files of type**, select **All Files** or **Text**. And that's it. Excel might take you through

Excel

CSV

Figure 14 *How you differentiate between CSV and regular Excel files in Windows Explorer is that CSV files huve what looks like a little a and 1 under the green x.*

a 3-Step Wizard to open the file, but it's simple. When you're finished with the file, just remember to save it as an Excel file.

Distribution Lists

Have you saved email addresses as part of a Group/Distribution List rather than as individual contacts? Want to know how to get them out of the Group and into your Contacts or Excel?

1. In Contacts or your Address Book, click open the **Group / Distribution** list.

2. Select **Copy to Folder** (Figure 15).

3. Click on the **Inbox** (Figure 16).

4. It will open a new email with the distribution list in the content of the email (Figure 17).

5. Copy this information from the body of the email, open a new **Excel** spreadsheet and paste it.

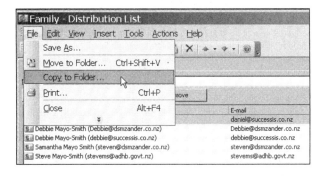

Figure 15 *To move Distribution List information to Excel, open the Group, and select Copy to Folder.*

6. If you want to bring them back to **Contacts** as all individual contacts, you would **Import** them back. So **Save** the **Excel** file (good tip – name the column headings the same as they're named in Contacts). Open Contacts and select **File, Import** and follow the Wizard. You'll have to **Map the Custom fields** (in other words you need to tell Outlook where to put this new information).

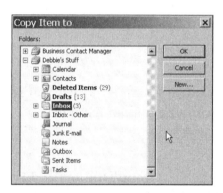

Figure 16 *It asks you where to copy it to. Select Inbox.*

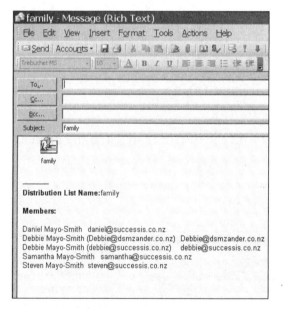

Figure 17 *Copy to Folder will put the entire Distribution List in the content of an email which you can copy and paste into Excel. To create individual contacts, follow step 6 above.*

Do you AutoComplete?

This wonderful function will guess to whom you're trying to address an email to by bringing up names beginning with the same letter/s that you typed so far. Select the one you want.

HOW DO I TURN ON AUTOCOMPLETE?

1. On the **Tools** menu, click **Options**.

2. Click **E-mail Options** and then click **Advanced E-mail Options**.

3. Under **When sending a message,** select the **Automatic name checking** and **Suggest names while completing To, Cc, and Bcc fields** check boxes.

GOT TOO MANY NAMES IN AUTOCOMPLETE?

To delete an AutoComplete suggestion:

1. Start to type the e-mail name of the AutoComplete suggestion you want to delete.

2. To delete the suggestion, press the DELETE key. If more than one suggestion appears, use the arrow keys to get to the suggestion you want to delete, and then press DELETE.

3. If you want to add an e-mail name back to AutoComplete, just send that person another email.

Getting the right Contact out of Outlook

For some strange reason (and it's beyond me how it happens technically) empty Address Books accumulate in Outlook, and sometimes Outlook forgets which is the correct one to use when you click open your Address Book icon, or search for a Contact while in your inbox.

If you ever tried to find the answer to solve this problem I bet it was like trying to find a needle in a haystack. The answer is that you must remind Outlook where to look first.

These steps change the address list that **Outlook** looks in first when you use the Address Book to look up a name.

HOW DO I TELL OUTLOOK WHERE TO LOOK FIRST TO VERIFY NAMES?

1. From inside the **Address Book,** click **Options** on the **Tools** menu (if the **Address Book** is closed, first click **Address Book** on the **Tools** menu).

2. The **Addressing** dialogue box appears.

3. Under **When sending mail,** check **Names in these address lists in the following order,** select the list that you want to show up first, and click the arrow in the dialogue box until that list appears first.

4. Did you see an address list here that you don't want Outlook to use when it verifies email addresses? No problem. Remove it by selecting it and clicking **Remove.**

THE ADDRESS BOOK ISN'T GIVING ME THE RIGHT ADDRESS LIST

These steps change the list that *you* look in first when you use the Address Book to look up a name.

1. Click **New** to create a new message.

2. In the message, click the **To** button. The **Select Names** dialogue box appears.
   Note which address list is displayed in the **Show Names from the box**.

3. Close the **Select Names** dialogue box, and close the message without saving it.

4. Click **Address Book**. From inside the Address Book, click **Options** on the **Tools** menu.
   The **Addressing** dialogue box appears.

5. Click the arrow next to the list, and select the list that you want to appear first.

6. Click **OK,** and close the Address Book.

202 CONQUER YOUR EMAIL OVERLOAD   visit www.debbiespeaks.co.nz

DON'T LIKE LAST NAMES FIRST? CHANGE HOW YOUR CONTACT NAMES ARE DISPLAYED

1. On the **Tools** menu in Outlook, click **E-mail accounts**.

2. Under **Directory**, select **View or change existing directories or address books**.

3. Click **Next**.

4. Make sure the **Outlook Address Book** is selected, and then click **Change**.

5. Click any contact list, and then, under **Show names by**, click either **File as (Smith, John)** or **First Last (John Smith)**.

6. Click **Close** and then click **Finish**.

7. Quit and restart Outlook.

This change will be applied to all of the contact lists in the Outlook Address Book. You cannot control the way other address books, such as a Global Address List on a Microsoft® Exchange Server or LDAP (Internet) directory, are sorted.

HOW DO I CREATE A NEW CONTACT LIST AND ADD IT TO MY ADDRESS BOOK?

By default, Outlook makes your main Contacts folder, which is always named Contacts, available from the Address Book. To create additional contacts folders and have them show up in the Address Book too, follow these steps:

1. On the **File** menu, point to **New**, and then click **Folder**.

The Create New Folder dialogue box opens.

2. In the **Name** box, type the name you want to call your new contact folder. Verify that **Contact Items** appears in the **Folder Contains** box.

3. Under **Select where to place the folder**, select a location for your new contacts folder. Click **OK**.

The new folder appears in the **Navigation Pane** under **My Contacts**.

4. To make sure that the new folder appears in your **Address Book**, right-click the folder, click **Properties**, and then click the **Outlook Address Book** tab. Verify that the **Show this folder as an e-mail Address Book** check box is selected, and then click **OK**.

CHAPTER EIGHTEEN

Help! Contacts won't hold the information I need!

Solutions in this chapter

☑ Adding new fields for your information in Contacts

☑ Creating a new Contact form

All the fields available in your Outlook Contacts

When I went to investigate how many fields there were in an Outlook Contact, I was mightily surprised with the result!

Many of the fields are hidden because they're contained within the drop-down boxes, as shown in Figure 3 from Chapter Fifteen (page 171).

It was only by exporting my Contacts (Chapter Seventeen) to have a squiz at them that I saw the volume of fields available, as shown on the next page.

The 92 Fields in Contacts

Title	Business Phone	Email 2 Display Name
First Name	Business Phone 2	Email 3 Address
Middle Name	Callback	Email 3 Type
Last Name	Car Phone	Email 3 Display Name
Suffix	Company Main Phone	Gender
Company	Home Fax	Government ID Number
Department	Home Phone	Hobby
Job Title	Home Phone 2	Home Address PO Box
Business Street	ISDN	Initials
Business Street 2	Mobile Phone	Internet Free Busy
Business Street 3	Other Fax	Keywords
Business City	Other Phone	Language1
Business State	Pager	Location
Business Postal Code	Primary Phone	Manager's Name
Business Country	Radio Phone	Mileage
Home Street	TTYTDD Phone	Notes
Home Street 2	Telex	Office Location
Home Street 3	Account	Organizational ID Number
Home City	Anniversary	Other Address PO Box
Home State	Assistants Name	Priority
Home Postal Code	Billing Information	Private
Home Country	Birthday	Profession
Other Street	Business Address PO Box	Referred By
Other Street 2	Categories	Sensitivity
Other Street 3	Children	Spouse
Other City	Directory Server	User 1
Other State	Email Address	User 2
Other Postal Code	Email Type	User 3
Other Country	Email Display Name	User 4
Assistants Phone	Email 2 Address	Web Page
Business Fax	Email 2 Type	

If you would like different fields, you can customise Contacts by creating extra fields or even customising the Contact Form itself.

Customising your Contacts

HOW DO I CREATE A CUSTOM CONTACT FIELD?

1. On the **View** menu, point to **Arrange By**, point to **Current View**, and then click **Customize Current View** or click **Custom** (Figure 1).

2. Click **Fields** (Figure 2).

3. Click **New Field** and enter the information you want (Figure 3).

4. In the **Show these fields in this order** window on the right side of the **Show Fields** dialogue box, select your new field, and then use **Move Up** and **Move Down** to specify the display order (Figure 4). This will be where it 'lies' in your contact information line-up when you view it (Figure 5).

5. To see the field in individual contacts when you open them, select the **General** Tab and select from the drop-down list of **User defined fields in folder** (Figure 6).

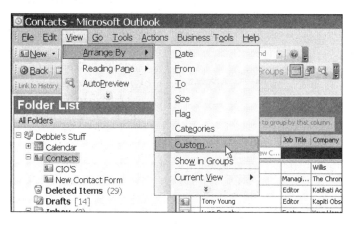

Figure 1 *To create a custom field, Click View > Arrange By > Custom.*

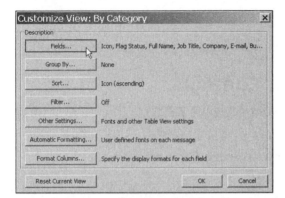

Figure 2 *Select Fields.*

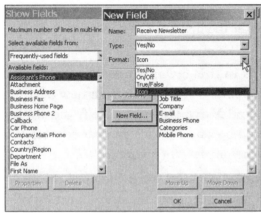

Figure 3 *Click New Fields, then enter the name you desire and also what type of field you want. There's a large selection. I've chosen to name my field Receive Newsletter and make it a simple yes/no field.*

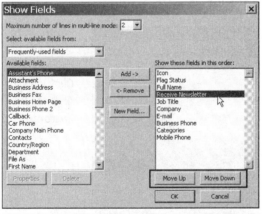

Figure 4 *In the Fields box on the right, select your new field, and then use Move Up and Move Down to specify the display order. This is to allocate where it will show when you view contact details in Outlook.*

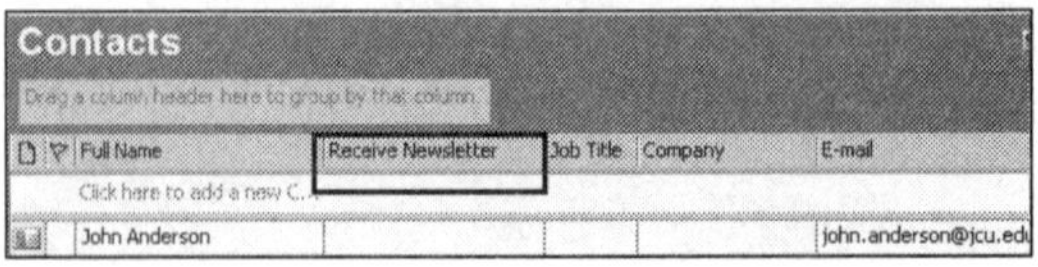

Figure 5 *Here's the new field in my Contacts.*

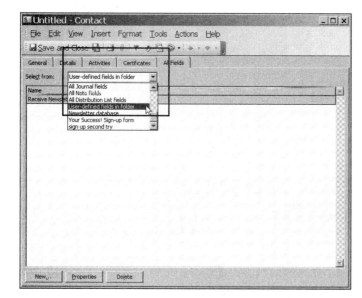

Figure 6 *You can find your new fields in the All Fields Tab when you select from the drop-down menu User defined fields.*

HOW DO I CREATE A NEW CONTACT FORM?

This is very advanced, and I recommend you have professional help with this. You'll probably need someone who knows how to code.

1. On the **Tools** menu, point to **Forms** and then click **Design a Form** (Figure 7).

2. Under **Standard Forms Library** select the form you want (**Contact**) – Figure 8.

3. Start working away with the **Field Chooser** and the **Control Toolboxes** (Figure 9).

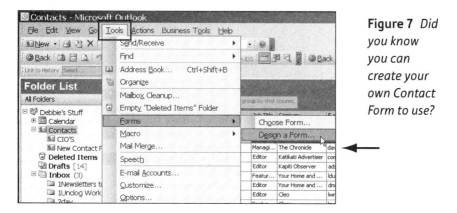

Figure 7 *Did you know you can create your own Contact Form to use?*

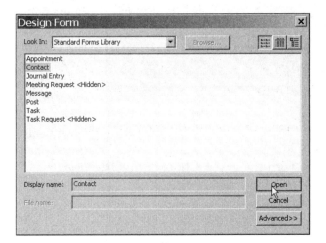

Figure 8 *Select Contacts from the Standard Forms Library.*

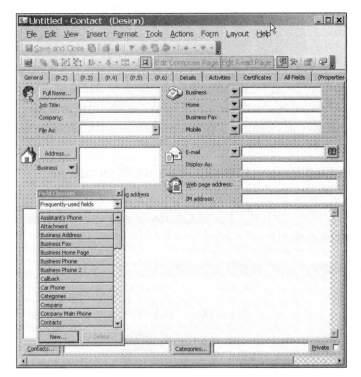

Figure 9 *And away you go. As this is too advanced a procedure to outline here, I suggest you read about it in your Help menu. Notice the dotted grey area. This tells you that you're working on the form.*

HOW DO I CREATE A NEW CONTACT FORM?

This is very advanced, and I recommend you have professional help with this. You'll probably need someone who knows how to code.

1. On the **Tools** menu, point to **Forms** and then click **Design a Form** (Figure 7).
2. Under **Standard Forms Library** select the form you want (**Contact**) – Figure 8.
3. Start working away with the **Field Chooser** and the **Control Toolboxes** (Figure 9).

CHAPTER NINETEEN

Help!
How can I get the most out of my Calendar?

Solutions in this chapter

☑ Appointments

☑ Meeting requests

☑ Events

☑ Makeovers, customising, shortcuts

☑ Additional calendars in Outlook 2003

☑ Making changes to how your Calendar works

☑ Printing a blank calendar

Calendar (only available in Outlook)

You might feel that the Calendar is of little or no use to you privately, or if you rarely have meetings. But let me beg to differ.

Just like you would check dates and write down appointments and events in a paper diary or organiser, you do so with your Calendar. Click on any day and time slot in it, and begin typing. Better yet, it fully integrates with email, Contacts, and other Outlook features.

One of the functions of the Calendar is to prompt and remind you. As in Tasks (Chapters Five and Fourteen), Calendar creates pop-up reminders when you have Outlook open. These reminders can be set to warn you anywhere from five minutes to two weeks in advance (I have mine set for two days).

Think laterally. It doesn't only *have* to be for meetings and appointments. How about having your Calendar remind/prompt you about upcoming:

- birthdays
- anniversaries
- children's school events
- parties
- get-togethers, social gatherings
- weddings
- school holidays
- holidays/vacation
- public holidays
- committee meetings
- important deadlines
- things to do
- reminders (like pick up the dry cleaning).

Calendar's limited terminology

The Calendar has just three settings (in its terminology):

1. **Appointments** (just you).

2. **Meetings** (with others – you can send them or receive meeting requests).

3. **Events** (all-day appointments).

Following from the ideas above, you can create a new 'appointment' – but in reality it can be your reminder of a friend's birthday, anniversaries, etc.

Appointments

HOW DO I CREATE AN APPOINTMENT?

While in Calendar, press CTRL+N.

or

1. On the **File** menu, point to **New**, and then click **Appointment**.

2. In the **Subject** box, type a description.

3. In the **Location** box, enter the location.

4. Enter start and end times.

5. Select any other options you want.

To make the appointment recur

6. Click **Recurrence**. Click the frequency (**Daily**, **Weekly**, **Monthly**, **Yearly**) with which the appointment recurs, and then select options for the frequency.

7. Click **OK**.

8. Click **Save and Close**.

WANT TO SELECT NON-ADJACENT DAYS?

1. Click **Day** on the **Standard** toolbar.

2. Click a date in the **Date Navigator** (small-sized calendar) to select that one day in the calendar.

3. Hold down CTRL while you click other dates in the **Date Navigator**.

You can show non-adjacent dates next to one another in the Calendar to make it clearer which day would be the best choice for a particular appointment.

To return to the current date, click the **Today** button on the **Standard** toolbar. To restore Day view, click **Day** on the **Standard** toolbar.

Top Tip

If you get an email that you'd like to create an Appointment from, drag & drop it into your calendar folder icon.

A new appointment opens with the email in the text box. Just set the time and date.

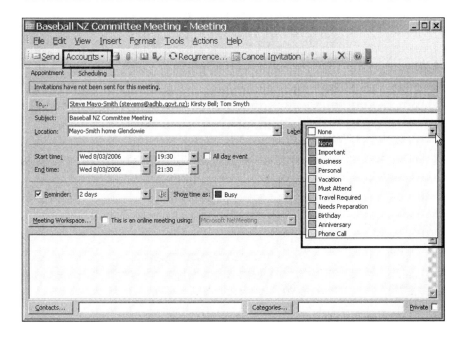

Figure 1 *Creating an Appointment. You can quickly change an appointment into a meeting to be scheduled by selecting the Scheduling tab and adding names. The Label tab has a drop-down selection of colour coded background settings to apply to that time slot if you desire.*

Colouring your appointments and meetings

Are ten colours enough for you? Colour the backgrounds of appointments and meetings as shown in Figure 1. These colours are visible in the Day, Week and Month views of **Calendar**.

Your manual or automatic colouring options

You can colour individual or recurring appointments and meetings manually, or you can use Rules to automatically colour them when they meet conditions you've set. An example is when a certain word is used in the subject, or a meeting request comes in from a particular person. Manual colouring always takes precedence over automatic colouring.

If you open another person's Calendar, or a Calendar stored in a public folder, you will see the colours that were assigned manually but not any automatic colouring. Automatic colouring can be seen only by the person who set it up.

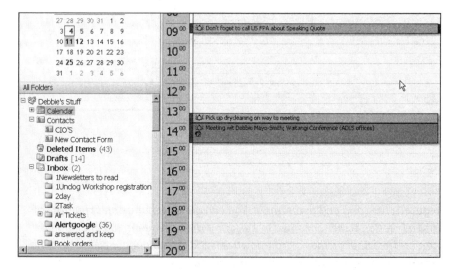

Figure 2 *Colour coding can help to categorise importance at a glance.*

Each colour comes with a label. You can change these labels to make them more meaningful to you. For example, you can change the label of the colour red from 'important' to 'urgent.'

HOW DO I CHANGE COLOUR LABELS?

1. In **Calendar**, click the **Calendar Coloring** icon, and then click **Edit Labels**.

2. Type the text you want to associate with each colour.

Displaying your availability status

When you view **Calendar** in **Day** or **Work Week** view, the pattern of the availability indicator to the left of any appointment or meeting displays your availability status for that time period: free, tentative, busy, or out of office.

Top Tip

Want to see your Calendar while you're looking at the Inbox?

In the Navigation Pane or Folder view, right-click the **Calendar** button, and then click **Open in New Window**.

Meeting Requests

HOW DO I CREATE A MEETING REQUEST?

As shown in Figure 3 you can turn an **Appointment** into a **Meeting** by selecting the **Schedule** Tab (right next to Appointment) and then selecting attendees by typing them in, **or** at the bottom left of the form there's an **Add Others** Tab. This opens your address book / contacts.

Conversely, while you're in the **Appointment** Tab there's a menu selection called **Invite Attendees**. Pressing this creates an email which you can then address (Figure 4). This will send them an email with a meeting request. The attendees can either accept or decline and the response comes back to you. Pretty neat for those who haven't used this function before.

For those within a corporation and on Microsoft® Exchange, you can share calendars and actually open and go into other's Calendars to check their availability. It's a convenient way to track your company events, conferences, business travel and employee holidays.

Top Tip

Share a calendar using Outlook and Windows SharePoint Services – MS Office Training:

http://office.microsoft.com/training/training.aspx?AssetID=RC0111870 01033

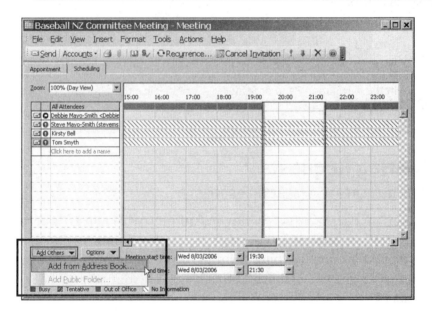

Figure 3 *Creating a Meeting Request – simply type in the name or click Add Others.*

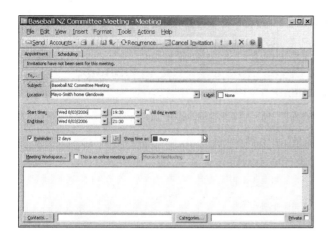

Figure 4
The Meeting Request creates an email that goes to the attendees. They can either accept or decline.

Events

HOW DO I CREATE AN EVENT?

An Event in Calendar is simply an all-day appointment. When you create an Appointment, simply check the **All day event** box next to the date. The Time of day setting disappears. You can opt to show the time as **Out of office**.

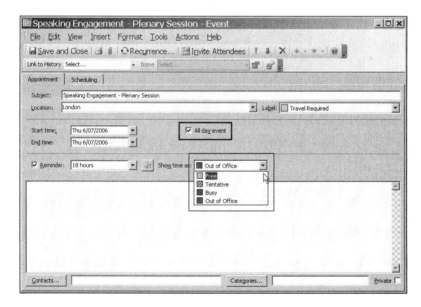

Figure 5 *Creating an Event is as simple as ticking a box. An event is viewed by your Calendar as an entire day occurrence, and the whole day will be blocked out.*

Making Calendar work the way *you* want

HOW DO I CHANGE THE LOOK OF MY CALENDAR?

There are many ways you can customise in Options.

1. Select the **Tools** menu.

2. Select **Options**.

3. In the Calendar section before you click **Calendar Options**, you might want to change when you're prompted with Calendar reminders (Figure 6).

4. Select **Calendar Options**.

Top Tip

Did you know you can use phrases such as 'tomorrow' or 'next Monday', and Outlook automatically inserts the correct date when you're setting an appointment?.

HOW DO I PREVIEW OR VIEW MY CALENDAR ITEMS?

Just like your other Outlook Folders, you can AutoPreview or have a Preview/Reading Pane open for your Calendar appointments, meetings and events.

1. In **Calendar**, on the **View** menu, point to **Reading Pane/ Preview**

or

2. In **Calendar**, on the **View** menu, point to **Arrange By Current View**.

3. Select **Day/Week/Month**, and **View with AutoPreview**.

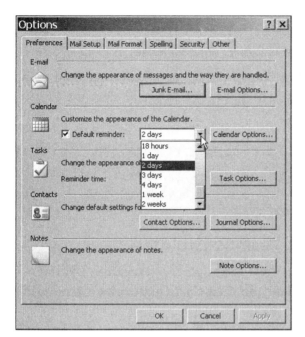

Figure 6 *Select when you want to be reminded of your appointments, meetings and events.*

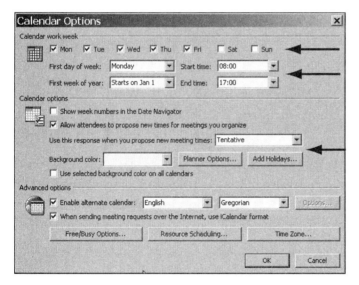

Figure 7 *Changes you can make to customise the Calendar to your needs.*

Some ideas on changes you can make

WANT OUTLOOK TO OPEN WITH YOUR CALENDAR?

1. On the **Tools** menu, click **Options,** and then click the **Other** tab.

2. Under **General**, click **Advanced Options**.

3. Next to **Startup** in this folder, click **Browse**.

4. In the **Select Folder** dialogue box, select **Calendar**, and then click **OK** three times to accept the change and close the open dialogue boxes.

 Top Tip
Want to go to a date in the future? Hit CTRL+G.

CHANGE THE DAY/WEEK/MONTH VIEW

1. In **Calendar**, on the **View** menu point to **Arrange By**, then point to **Current View** and then click **Customize Current View**.

2. Click **Other Settings**.

3. Do any of the following:

   - to change the day display, change the **Time Font, Font,** and **Time scale**

   - to display appointment end times, under **Week** or **Month**, select the **Show end time** check box

   - to display weekends together, select the **Compress weekend days** check box

   - to display appointment times as miniature clocks, under **Week** or **Month**, select the **Show time as clocks** check box.

CHANGE THE FONT

1. On the **Tools** menu, click **Options**, and then click the **Other** tab.

2. Click **Advanced Options**.

3. Under **Appearance Options**, click **Font**.

4. Select the font and other options you want.

SHOW WEEK NUMBERS

1. On the **Tools** menu, click **Options**.

2. Click **Calendar Options**.

3. To display **week numbers**, select the **Show week numbers in the Date Navigator** check box.

TURN ON OR OFF BOLD DATES

1. In **Calendar,** on the **View** menu, point to **Arrange By**, then point to **Current View** and then click **Customize Current View**.

2. Click **Other Settings**.

3. Under **General settings**, clear or select the **Bolded dates in Date Navigator represent days containing items** check box.

SET WORK WEEK OPTIONS

This is good if you're not a 9–5, Monday to Friday, kind of person.

1. On the **Tools** menu, click **Options**.

2. Click **Calendar Options**.

3. Do any of the following:

   • to select the days of your work week, select the check boxes next to the days of the week you want

   • to set the first day of the week, in the **First day of week** box, click the day you want

   • to set the first week of the year, in the **First week of year** box, click the option you want

   • to set the first and last hours of your workday, enter times in the **Start time** box and the **End time** box.

Top Tip

Appointment time change?

Drag it to a new date or time in your Calendar or in the date picker.

CHANGE THE NUMBER OF DAYS DISPLAYED IN CALENDAR

In **Calendar**, on the toolbar click any of the following options:

- **Day**
- **Week**
- **Work Week**
- **Month**

and make the changes you want.

CHANGE THE BACKGROUND COLOUR

1. On the **Tools** menu, click **Options**, and then click **Calendar Options**.

2. In the **Background color** list, click the colour you desire.

   - The colour you choose is applied to **Day** and **Work Week** views. **Week** and **Month** views use system background colours, which by default are grey and white.

   - The colour you choose is applied to weekday hours. A darker version of the background colour is applied to night and weekend hours.

Top Tip

One of the new features of 2003 is your ability to create **multiple calendars**.

The example I used in Figure 8 is a calendar I've created containing my old speaking engagements. I use this to see what time of year my clients hold their conferences so that about one and a half years later I can send an email asking if I may submit a proposal for their next one. Take this idea and apply it to your business.

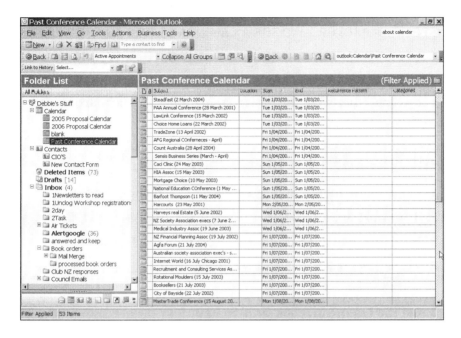

Figure 8 *One of the different views you can select is by appointments rather than by date (View > Current View menu).*

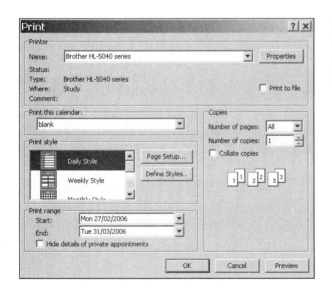

Figure 9 *There are several choices for printing a blank calendar.*

1. In **Calendar,** on the **File** menu, click **Save as Web Page**.

2. Under **Options,** select the **Use background graphic** check box, and then type the path to the graphic or click **Browse** to choose the path.

How do I print a blank calendar?

1. On the **File** menu, point to **New** and then click **Folder**.

2. Type a name for the folder.

3. In the **Folder contains** list, click **Calendar Items**.

4. In the **Select where to place the folder** list, click **Calendar,** and then click **OK**.

5. On the **Go** menu, click **Folder List**.

6. In the **Folder List,** click the new folder you just created.

7. On the File menu, point to **Page setup,** and then click the print style you want.

8. Select the print style options you want, and then click **Print**.

Great Calendar Keyboard Shortcuts

ACTION	KEYBOARD SHORTCUT
Change Calendar to Week	ALT+HYPHEN
Change Calendar to Month	ALT+EQUAL SIGN
Change Calendar to see specific number of days	ALT+ number of days (for example, ALT+5 shows five days)
Move to a specific date (or a far-away date)	CTRL+G
Create a new Appointment	CTRL+SHIFT+A or CTRL+N
Create a new Meeting Request	CTRL+SHIFT+Q
Delete a Meeting Request	CTRL+D
Send a Meeting Request	ALT+S
Save and close an Appointment	ALT+S
Accept a Meeting Request	ALT+C
Tentatively accept a Meeting Request	ALT+N
Decline a Meeting Request	ALT+D

CHAPTER TWENTY

Help!
Are there any more tips on
using my Calendar?

Solutions in this chapter

☑ 25 more great Calendar ideas and tips

☑ Do's and don'ts for handling meeting requests

---

25 more great Calendar ideas and tips
How do I . . .

---

1. SCHEDULE A MEETING WITH SOMEONE IN ANOTHER TIME ZONE?

Just add the time zone to Outlook.

a. On the **Tools** menu, click **Options**, and then click the **Preferences** tab.

b. Click **Calendar Options**, click **Time Zone**, and then select the **Show an additional time zone** check box.

c. Click the time zone you want in the **Time Zone** list.

---

2. QUICKLY CREATE AN APPOINTMENT WHILE IN CALENDAR?

a. Click the day of the appointment on the calendar. If it's for half an hour, double-click on the specific time of the appointment. A new Appointment opens pre-set for that time frame, *or*

b. Drag your mouse over the block of time when the appointment occurs. A new Appointment opens pre-set to begin and end with your selected time. Then type a description.

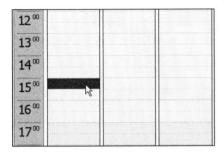

Figure 1 *When you want to set an Appointment, you can double-click the time on the day and a new half-hour appointment will open ready for you to enter the details.*

3. CONTACT MEETING ATTENDEES WITH A REMINDER OR OTHER MESSAGE?

Open the original meeting request, click the **Actions** menu, and then click **New Message to Attendees.**

4. USE MY EMAIL SIGNATURE IN MEETING REQUESTS?

On the **Insert** menu, click **Signature** and then click the signature you desire.

5. QUICKLY COPY AN APPOINTMENT IN YOUR CALENDAR?

Hold down CTRL and drag the Appointment to a new time or date.

6. ABBREVIATE WHEN ENTERING MEETING TIMES?

When you enter Appointments in the Calendar, you can save time by typing abbreviations and allowing Outlook to fill in the rest.

For example, if you want to enter a 9:00 a.m. meeting, open a new meeting request and then type 900 am into the time box.

You can also use phrases such as 'tomorrow' or 'next Monday', and Outlook automatically inserts the correct date. Just type that into the start time.

7. GET CONSENSUS ON A MEETING TIME?

Let invitees propose new meeting times.

a. On the **Tools** menu, click **Options**.

b. Click **Preferences** and then click **Calendar Options**.

c. In the **Calendar Options** section, select the **Allow attendees to propose new meeting times for meetings you organise check box**.

8. HAVE FROM 1 TO 10 DAYS SHOW IN CALENDAR?

In Calendar view, press ALT+*number*, where *number* represents the number of days to show in the view, between 1 and 9. Use 0 for a 10-day view.

9. TRACK ALL ATTENDEES EVEN IF I CAN'T SEND THEM A MEETING REQUEST?

On the **Scheduling** tab, in the **All Attendees** list, click the envelope next to the name, and then click **Don't send meeting to this attendee**.

10. QUICKLY CHANGE AN APPOINTMENT INTO AN ALL-DAY EVENT?

In the Calendar, in Day view, drag the appointment (from its appointed time slot) up to the day heading.

11. QUICKLY CREATE AN ALL-DAY EVENT IN CALENDAR?

Click the **Day** heading that you want, and then type the name of the Event.

If the Event lasts several days, click the first **Day** heading, drag across all days, and then type the Event name.

12. AUTOMATICALLY ADD HOLIDAYS TO MY CALENDAR?

On the **Tools** menu, click **Options**, click **Calendar Options**, and then click **Add Holidays**. Select the country you're in, of course.

13. SET AN APPOINTMENT TO REPEAT?

To do so, set it as recurring.

In the Appointment, click the **Actions** menu, and then click **Recurrence**.

14. LET OUTLOOK FIND A MEETING TIME WHEN ALL ATTENDEES ARE AVAILABLE?

You must be on a Microsoft® Exchange Server for this.

On the **Scheduling** tab, type the names of the attendees in the **All Attendees** list, and then click **AutoPick Next**.

15. QUICKLY SEE WHEN CONFERENCE ROOMS IN MY BUILDING ARE AVAILABLE?

You must be on a Microsoft® Exchange Server for this.

On the **Scheduling** tab of a new Meeting Request, add all rooms as resources to the **All Attendees** list. After you find a conference room that is available, delete the others.

16. QUICKLY SWITCH BETWEEN VIEWING A DAY, WEEK, OR MONTH IN CALENDAR?

Click the **Day**, click to the left of the **Week** row, or click the **Day of the week** heading.

17. QUICKLY DISPLAY SEVERAL DAYS SIDE BY SIDE IN CALENDAR?

In the **Date Picker** (the mini calendar), drag over the dates that you want to view, and those days will show in your large calendar view.

18. CHANGE THE SUBJECT OF A MEETING OR APPOINTMENT?

In Calendar, click the Meeting or Appointment and then type the new subject.

19. CHANGE THE TIME PERIODS IN THE CALENDAR GRID?

You can change the default setting for 30-minute time slots to 5, 6, 10, 15, or 60-minute time slots.

a. Right-click the **Calendar**.

b. Click **Other Settings**.

c. Then click the number you want from the **Time Scale** list.

20. ATTACH AN AGENDA OR MEETING MINUTES TO A MEETING REQUEST?

If the agenda or minutes are in a file, you can attach the file to a Meeting Request. In the Meeting Request, on the Insert menu, click **File**, and then locate the file you want to attach.

21. QUICKLY SHARE MEETING NOTES WITH ATTENDEES?

Open the Meeting Request in Calendar, add the notes, save it, and then drag the item to your Inbox. Drag the meeting attendees names from the body of the email to the **To** box, and then send the email.

22. QUICKLY CREATE A MEETING REQUEST FROM A MEETING AGENDA?

Drag the file that contains the agenda to the **Calendar** button in the **Navigation Pane**, and then complete the Meeting Request.

23. AUTOMATICALLY OPEN SOMEONE ELSE'S INBOX OR CALENDAR?

You must be on Microsoft® Exchange to do this.

If you have permission, you can have Outlook automatically open another person's Inbox or Calendar when you start Outlook. Just leave the other person's folder open when you exit Outlook.

24. AVOID RECEIVING MEETING REQUEST RESPONSES?

If you're sending a Meeting Request to a large group and don't need or want responses, in the **Open New Meeting Request**, on the **Actions** menu, click **Request Responses**. Specify your meeting information, and then send the Meeting Request.

25. SHOW SATURDAY AND SUNDAY IN SEPARATE BOXES IN MY MONTHLY CALENDAR?

To show weekend days in separate boxes in the **Month** view, right-click anywhere in **Calendar** view, and then click **Other Settings**. Clear the **Compress weekend days** check box.

Meeting Request Top Tips

1. DO IT

Accept, Accept as Tentative, or Decline each Meeting Request that you receive, especially if it is an update to a Meeting Request that you previously accepted. By taking action on the Meeting Request, you prevent the meetings that you want to attend from being accidentally deleted. Be sure not to delete a Meeting Request outright, because this is one way that meetings get 'lost'.

2. DON'T FORGET TO KEEP EVERYONE POSTED!

If you change it, update it. After modifying one of your own Meeting requests, remember to click **Send Update** to send the updated request to all recipients.

3. LET EVERYONE KNOW IF IT'S OFF

If you need to cancel a meeting, delete the meeting from your calendar, click **Send cancellation and delete meeting**, and then send the cancellation to everyone you invited.

4. CONVERT, DON'T FORWARD

If you want to create a meeting from an Appointment on your calendar, open the Appointment, click **Invite Attendees**, and then select the people you want to invite. This converts the Appointment to a Meeting Request. Don't simply forward your Appointment to the people you want to invite to the meeting.

5. WORKING ON TWO COMPUTERS?

If you run Outlook on two computers and accept a meeting while using one of them, don't delete the Meeting Request from the Inbox on the other computer. If the request is still there, accept it again. Deleting a request on one computer after accepting it on another computer can cause the meeting to disappear from your calendar.

6. KEEP YOUR MEETING NOTES ELSEWHERE

As a meeting attendee, don't add your own private notes to the body of a Meeting request in your calendar. If the organiser updates the meeting, your notes get lost.

7. DON'T MOVE MEETING REQUESTS

Don't move a Meeting Request from your Inbox to a different folder before you accept or decline the request, or before the meeting appears in your calendar.

Soon after a Meeting Request arrives in your Inbox, a piece of Outlook code automatically adds the meeting to your calendar and marks it as tentative. This is a fail-safe to keep you from missing the meeting in case you don't see the request in your Inbox. However, the sniffer doesn't reply to the meeting organiser. You still need to do that by Accepting, Accepting as Tentative, or Declining the request.

If you or a Rule you create moves an incoming Meeting Request from your Inbox before the sniffer can process the request, the meeting never appears in your calendar, and you might miss the meeting.

8. THERE IS ALWAYS ROOM FOR ONE MORE

If you are the meeting organiser and you want to invite another person after sending the original meeting request, add the person to the attendee list (the **To** box) of the original meeting series or occurrence, and then send an update to all attendees.

Never just forward an existing meeting series or occurrence to the additional person you want to invite.

9. REMOVE IT RIGHT

If you receive a meeting cancellation, click **Remove from Calendar** to remove the meeting from your calendar. Don't just delete the cancellation from your Inbox; this won't remove the meeting from your calendar.

10. BE CAREFUL WITH DISTRIBUTION LISTS (GROUPS)

Try to avoid sending Meeting Requests to Distribution Lists, particularly ones that you are a member of. If you need to send a Meeting Request to a Distribution List, don't expand the list in the **To** box.

11. START OVER

If a meeting series requires several changes – a new organiser, a different frequency or time slot, the addition or removal of attendees – just cancel the series and create a new one. Don't try to modify the original meeting request.

CHAPTER TWENTY ONE

Help!
How can I improve the way
I view things?

Solutions in this chapter

☑ Looking at Outlook folders in different **Views**

☑ Customising **Toolbars**

☑ 9 more great customisation tips

Have it your way

- Inherited a computer?
- Someone else set up Outlook for you?
- Never have time to experiment?
- Didn't know you *could* experiment?

Busy bees

We're always so busy doing our jobs, or multi-tasking, that we rarely stop to smell the roses. Nor do we stop to take the time to see if there's a better way of doing things. I'm also going to hit you with this favourite saying of mine: 'You don't know what you don't know until someone shows you.'

As you learn more functions in your software, perhaps a change will come over you. You'll know that you can do almost anything with the software and might start looking for answers in Help menus, drop-down boxes, and the like, to find that shortcut you know **must** exist!

I always suggest to people that if they want to learn a new software, go to a large bookstore and grab all the books on the subject (such as Excel, or FrontPage, or Photoshop). Sit down and start browsing through them to get the right fit of book. Some are pictorial – teaching by screenshots. Some are exceedingly text-heavy. Some instruct through lists and bullet points. Then purchase the one most suitable to your learning style.

Does it fit you well?

Well, does your Outlook view suit you? Did you know that the Outlook folders all have different ways that you can view them, and that you can also customise like mad?

Depending on your job, your correspondence, your home use, and your personality, one view might be suited to you much more than another. For example – wherever I go I see people with their contacts showing in Card view. I had that view for years, because that was how it was in a few offices I worked in and how my husband set it up for me. But how I hate that view! I've switched for the past few years to Company view. It suits me to a T!

That's just the beginning of the changes you can make.

Contacts viewed differently

So I'm going to be boring, and make you take the time to sample different views, by doing a series of screenshots with Contacts as an example. Then I'll list some tips for you. For brevity's sake, I won't go through *all* the folders, but the next time you go into Outlook, have a play, and look at the standard views available to you in your Inbox, Tasks, Contacts and Calendar. As I said, each one of these can be further customised (see Figure 1).

To change your view in any of the folders, you select the **View** menu, **Current View**. A drop-down list will appear, as in Figure 2.

The standard choices in Contacts are:

- Address Cards (Figure 3).
- Detailed Address Cards.
- Phone List (Figure 4).
- By Company (Figure 5).
- By Category (Figure 6).
- By Location.
- By Follow Up Flag.

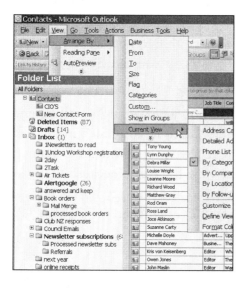

Figure 1 *Changing your view in Contacts is as simple as clicking on View > Current View.*

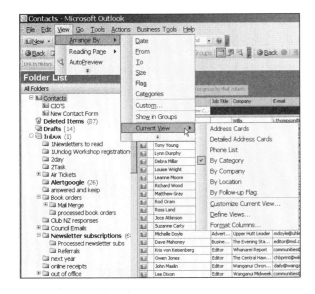

Figure 2 *When you customise views, you can even change the font and its size. I always make mine bigger than standard (it comes in 8 point; I change it to 10) to help these poor old eyes of mine. It's View > Arrange By > Customize Current View > Other Settings (not shown in this illustration).*

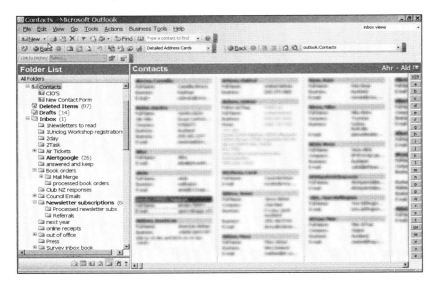

Figure 3 *Address Cards and Detailed Address Cards are similar. Detailed Address Cards will show content of text fields if any (that big empty space in a Contact). Note: Illustation is blurred for privacy reasons.*

.

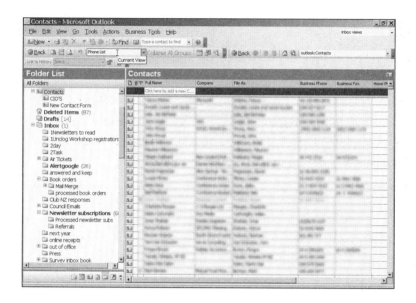

Figure 4 *Contacts arranged by Phone List. Useful if you needed to print off a list for telephoning. Note: Illustration is blurred for privacy reasons.*

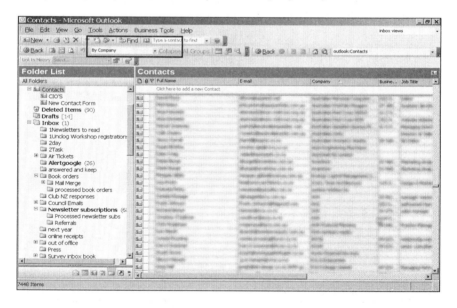

Figure 5 *This is how I always keep mine – by Company. It's a nice simple list, and you can see quite a few at a time. Don't forget the Find a Contact box will find anyone for you quick as a wink. You only need to type in a few letters, part of an email address or company name. Note: Illustration is blurred for privacy reasons.*

Top Tip

Don't forget about AutoComplete. It not only works in Contacts (Find a Contact), it works for every email you create and send too.

All you do is type in a piece of the name, company or email address. It brings up a list of suggested contacts to use. You double-click the correct one. AutoComplete saves a lot of time scrolling, or having to double-click the To column and look for the correct email address.

HOW DO I CREATE A VIEW FROM SCRATCH?

1. On the **View** menu, point to **Arrange By**, point to **Current View**, and then click **Define Views**.

2. Click **New**.

3. In the **Name of new view** box, type a name.

4. In the **Type of view** box, select the view type you want (table, timeline, day/week/month, card, or icon) to determine how information will be arranged and formatted in your new view.

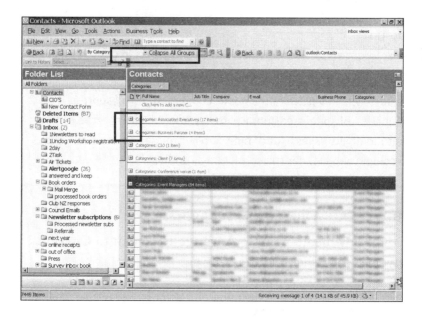

Figure 6 *Arranged by Category is handy when you need to contact that segment of your contacts. Here I have Group selected and the contacts within the Groups collapsed. To open, just click on the little plus sign in the upper left-hand corner of the category, or select Collapse all Groups on the menu. Note: Illustration is blurred for privacy reasons.*

5. To change where the view be available, select an option under **Can be used on**.

6. Click **OK**.

7. In the **Customize View:** *view name* dialogue box, select the options you want to use.

8. When you finish selecting options, click **OK**.

9. To use the view immediately, click **Apply View**.

Neat tips on customising your toolbars

HOW DO I CREATE A VIEW BASED ON A STANDARD VIEW?

1. Switch to the view you want to base the new view on.

2. On the **View** menu, point to **Arrange By**, and then click **Custom**.

3. For each type of change you want to make, click a button, and then select the options you want.

4. When you are finished making changes, close the **Customize View:** *view name* dialogue box.

5. On the **View** menu, point to **Arrange By**, point to **Current View**, and then click **Define Views**.

6. In the **Views for folder** *folder name* box, click **Current view settings**.

7. Click **Copy**.

8. In the **Name of new view** box, enter a name.

9. To change where the view will be available, click an option under **Can be used on**.

HOW DO I CREATE A CUSTOMISED TOOLBAR?

Maybe the toolbar choices Microsoft® Office offers just don't suit your needs. Maybe you want a toolbar that is for drawing, formatting, and creating formulas. Instead of having to have all three toolbars showing, create one of your own.

1. On the **Tools** menu, click **Customize**.

2. Click the **Toolbars** tab.

3. Click **New**.

4. In the **Toolbar name** box, type the name you want, and then click **OK**.

5. Click the **Commands** tab.

6. Click a category in the **Categories** box.

7. Drag the command you want from the **Commands** box to the toolbar you just created.

8. When you have added all the buttons and menus you want, click **Close**.

HOW DO I CHANGE A PICTURE ON A BUTTON?

1. On the **Tools** menu, click **Customize**.

2. Click the **Commands** tab, and, with the **Customize** dialogue box open, click the button on the toolbar.

3. Click **Modify Selection**, point to **Change Button Image**, and then click an image.

HOW DO I HIDE SCREENTIPS ON BUTTONS?

ScreenTips are those notes that pop up when you rest your mouse pointer on a button.

1. On the **Tools** menu, click **Customize**.

2. Click the **Options** tab.

3. Clear the checkbox for **Show ScreenTips on toolbars**.

Want more ScreenTips? Check the box that says **Show shortcut keys in ScreenTips**.

HOW DO I INCREASE THE SIZE OF A TOOLBAR BUTTON OR DROP-DOWN LIST BOX?

1. On the **Tools** menu, click **Customize**.

2. Click the **Options** tab.

3. Select the **Large icons** check box.

HOW DO I CHANGE THE WIDTH OF DROP-DOWN LIST BOXES?

1. On the **Tools** menu, click **Customize**.

2. With the **Customize** dialogue box open, click the list box you want to change – for example, the **Font** or **Font Size** box on the **Formatting** toolbar.

3. Point to the left or right edge of the box. When the pointer changes to a double-headed arrow, drag the edge of the box to change its width.

HOW DO I TURN SOUND ON (OR OFF)?

1. On the **Tools** menu, click **Options**, and then click the **General** tab.

2. Select or clear the **Provide feedback with sound** check box.

I MESSED UP! HOW DO I GET BACK MY ORIGINAL SETTINGS?

1. On the **View** menu, point to **Toolbars**, and then click **Customize**.

2. Do one or more of the following:

   - To restore original settings for a menu:

     a. with the **Customize** dialogue box open, right-click the menu you want to restore, and then click **Reset** on the shortcut menu

     b. on the **Customize** dialogue box, click **Close**.

   - To restore original buttons and menus and a built-in toolbar:

     a. click the **Toolbars** tab

     b. in the Toolbars box, click the name of the toolbar you want to restore

     c. click **Reset**.

9 more great customisation tips
How do I . . .

1. START OUTLOOK IN A FOLDER OTHER THAN INBOX?

On the **Tools** menu, click **Options** and then click the **Other** tab. In the **Advanced Options** dialogue box, set the **Startup Folder** that you want.

2. ADD A TIME ZONE?

Add a second time zone and switch between time zones for all Windows®-based programs. Click **Swap Time Zones** in the **Time Zone** dialogue box (**Tools** > **Options** > **Calendar Options**).

3. RE-USE CUSTOM VIEWS?

If you change a view by adding columns or changing the format and want to save it for re-use, type a new view name in the **Current View** box on the **Advanced** toolbar, and then press ENTER.

4. SEE DETAILS ABOUT THE VIEW I AM USING?

For details such as which fields are in place and if the view is filtered or sorted, right-click the table header and then click **Customize Current View**.

5. ADJUST MY VIEW FILTER SETTINGS? (I'M MISSING SOME ITEMS)

Items that don't match the filter settings won't appear. To remove the filter, on the **View** menu, point to **Arrange By**, point to **Current View**, and then click **Customize Current View**. Click **Filter**, and then click **Clear All**.

6. GET A CUSTOM VIEW OF MY INFORMATION, SORTED OR FILTERED IN A DIFFERENT WAY?

On the View menu, point to **Arrange By**, point to **Current View**, and then click **Define Views**.

7. SAVE TIME WHEN I CHANGE PRINT STYLES?

If you frequently change a print style before printing, create a custom print style instead. On the **File** menu, point to **Page Setup**, and then click **Define Print Styles**.

8. ACCESS ANY OUTLOOK FOLDER FROM MY WINDOWS° DESKTOP?

Create a shortcut to an Outlook folder on the Windows® desktop by dragging the folder from Outlook to your Windows desktop. Make sure you press CTRL before you release the mouse button (if you don't, it will move it there instead of copying it). When you double-click the new shortcut, Outlook will open to that folder.

9. QUICKLY REMOVE A COLUMN FROM THE VIEW?

Drag the column title away from the column heading row until an X appears, and then release the mouse button.

CHAPTER TWENTY-TWO

Help!
What on earth is this new
Business Contact Manager
in Outlook 2003?

Solutions in this chapter

☑ What is a **Business Contact Management** system?

☑ Do I need it?

Business Contact Manager

This is something brand new in Microsoft® Office 2003. It comes free with the Professional and Small Business editions (however, it is **NOT** on office networked computers).

It supplements the existing Outlook features to form a contact management system akin to one you would normally purchase separately, such as ACT or Goldmine.

You're probably thinking, 'So what is a contact management system and do I need it? Should I use it?'

Even more than the name implies, contact management systems help you in at least ten ways:

1. **Email**

2. **Contacts (Address Book)**

3. **Calendar**

4. **Communication history**
   Records of how and when you interact with a contact. Be it by email, phone, letters – they are automatically (or for some items manually) recorded with the contact. So you can always review communication streams and activity with each person, client, prospective client, account, etc.

5. **Multiple staff dealing with contacts**
   The contact files in these systems (if they're networked) don't stand alone. Rather they show your company interaction as a whole (all your employees) with these contacts.

6. **Knowledge**
   Because so much information is recorded, you develop a knowledge base for each client, prospect, account, etc.

7. **Staff turnover doesn't affect you as deeply**
   Because you've had communication history recorded automatically (and manually), the knowledge is left in your contact management system when an employee leaves rather than walking out the door with them.

8. **Sales forecast**
   If you are in an industry with large dollar-value (and thus perhaps less frequent sales), a benefit of these systems is their ability to forecast sales (if you enter the details of both your activity and the probabilities that you will be successful).

9. **Reporting**
   They can generate a multitude of reports, such as sales and staff activity.

10. **Tracking**
    They can track activities and opportunities.

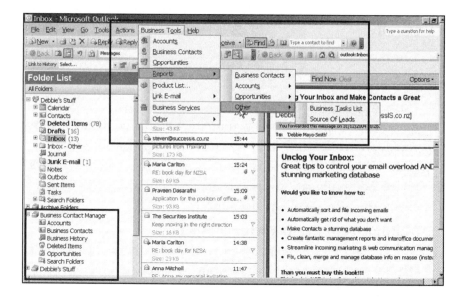

Figure 1 *Business Contact Manager lives below your Search Folders and has its own menu and toolbar.*

Quick comparison chart

Keep in mind that other contact management systems integrate with Microsoft® Office and often use all the features of Outlook. Business Contact Manager is fully integrated into Outlook. Think of them as a two-part team, working together. Business Contact Manager has its own menu system under **Business Tools**.

Feature	Others (ACT, Goldmine)	Outlook	Business Contact Manager
Email	✓	✓	✓
Contacts – individual	✓	✓	
Contacts – accounts	✓		✓
Calendar	✓	✓	
Tasks	✓	✓	
Link history	✓		✓
Product information & pricing	✓		✓
Sales forecasts	✓		✓
Sales tracking	✓		✓
Reporting	✓		✓
(Sales) Opportunities	✓		✓

So what are the Business Contact Manager features?

Accounts

This is nice, a two-level contact system. **Accounts** (the company) along with **Business Contacts** (the employees you have listed as contacts). Think 'corporate' apple tree. The Account is the tree, and all the people working within it, your contacts, are the apples. In my example in Figure 2, I have an Account called ICMI Speakers Bureau. Individually I have five Business Contacts that I have attached to that Account. You can use the information you've stored in Accounts to check the standing of a specific account, filter or sort Account information, or create status reports. You can also view all the History – or the correspondence with all the people within that Account.

Business Contacts

The same as Contacts, but (as mentioned above) they can be grouped under Accounts. You might consider storing your personal contacts in Outlook, and business ones in Business Contacts.

History

As you communicate with your Business Contacts – by sending them emails or setting appointments – Business Contact Manager automatically links these items to the History log for the appropriate

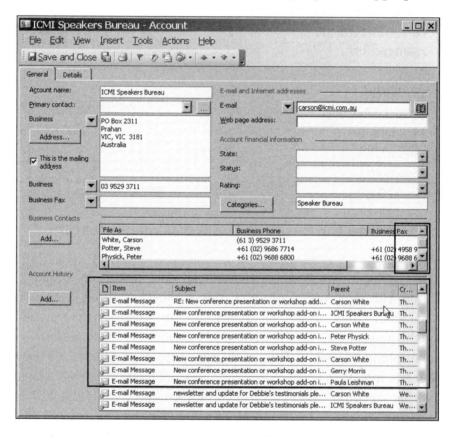

Figure 2 *My ICMI Speakers' Bureau Account. You can see that I have several Business Contacts listed within this Account, and the communication history is being logged not only with the individual contacts but also within the Account itself.*

Business Contact or Account.

You can also manually link phone-call records, tasks, notes, opportunities, and files to the appropriate records. At any time, you can sort or filter the log to view specific History items such as emails or tasks.

Reports
You can create Reports based on information from Accounts, Business Contacts, Opportunities, or Other. Reports are found by clicking on **Business Tools > Reports**. The reports look just like Access Reports (gee, I wonder why?). You can tailor them a bit, but only a bit. Reports can be printed, and when saved are in Word document format.

Opportunities
Prospects, leads or sales in progress. You can key in your products and their prices, and then assign a percentage chance of a proposal (**Opportunity**) coming through and track potential future income. Figure 3 shows the Reports you can generate for your opportunities.

Do I need it?

It depends. It depends on your business needs, your communication programme, and if you actually want a full-blown contact management system or simply a marketing database.

Look again at the contact management functions below. Which do you really need? While it might sound wonderful having account history, will you ever look at it? Sales activity reports sound dandy, but the reports are only as good as your staff diligently keying in all that information. What will you use that is *above and beyond* what you would normally have available with Outlook. If you have MYOB, Quicken or a stand-alone accounting package, these progams probably do (or can) generate a lot of these reports for you already.

1. Accounts.
2. Email history with each contact.
3. Product information and pricing.
4. Sales forecasting.
5. Sales tracking.
6. Reporting on leads and sales opportunities.

The question is, will you use it and do you need it?

With my business Successful Internet Strategies, we have an enormous number of Contacts because we have a monthly online newsletter that goes to anyone that asks to be subscribed. It exceeds 13,000.

Comparatively, we have fewer clients that fall into different categories – purchased book, attended workshop, conference presentation, consulting. We can track all that on our marketing database.

We do not require a full-blown contact management system. What we need at SIS is a *great* informative marketing database.

Conversely, if I were in financial services or ran a company where we didn't do a monthly newsletter, or there were several people nurturing a sale along or communicating with clients, or if I had high employee turnover, I'd be keen to use a contact management system. In these circumstances, the total picture of client information is paramount.

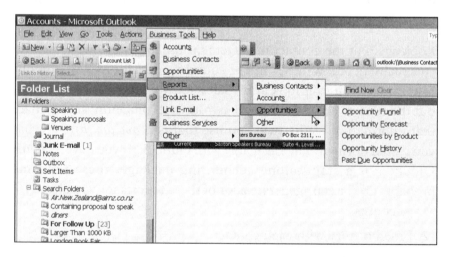

Figure 3 *There's a variety of reports you can generate for Accounts, Business Contacts, Opportunities and Other.*

APPENDICES

Using the menu bar without your mouse

Learning the (enormous) tip below was a real epiphany for me! It was something that for years and years nagged at me, but I couldn't figure it out!

I always knew that all those underlined letters in any Microsoft® menu were telling me that that was the 'letter' to press to get to the shortcut. But I never knew how to get them to work.

Well, I hope you get as excited as I did when you learn this great keyboard shortcut tip below.

HOW DO I GET TO THE MENU AND COMMANDS WITH THE KEYBOARD?

1. You first place focus on the menu bar (the one with all the commands like File, Edit, View, Go, Tools, Actions . . .) by pressing the ALT key.
2. And the menu you want is then opened by pressing the underlined letter.
3. Additionally, you select a second command by simply pressing the next underlined letter (you don't have to press ALT again).

So ALT+ the underlined letter in the menu name will open that menu. For example, ALT+F opens the File menu. ALT+V opens the View menu. If you look at the top of your menus in any program, one letter will be underlined. By pressing ALT+ the letter, it opens that menu.

Then, when the particular menu is opened, each command in it will have another letter underlined. If you press that letter alone, it will activate the command. Let's say you press ALT+F for file. If you press 'P' next, the Print dialogue box opens.

Move along the toolbars by using tab or the arrow keys. When the focus is on the button you require, press enter to select it.

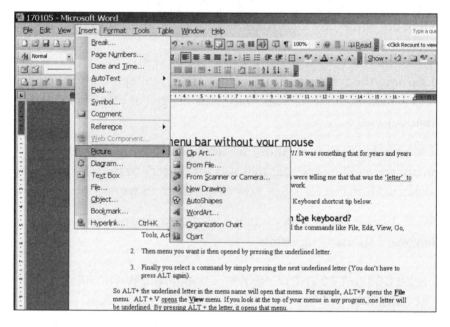

Figure 1 *While working on the manuscript, if I had wanted to insert a picture without using my mouse, I would press* ALT+I *(to open the Insert menu), then I'd press* 'P' *to get to the picture submenu, then I'd press* 'F' *to go to the file to get it.*

APPENDIX II

Moving around the text

Here are some jiffy keystrokes to move the insertion point around text, or to select text.

Press SHIFT+ any of the following keystrokes to select text. Remember CTRL+A to select all the text in a document.

To Move	Press Shift +	Action
Character	←	Left one character at a time
	→	Right one character at a time
Line	↓	Down one line at a time
	↑	Up one line at a time
	HOME	To the beginning of the current line of text
	END	To the end of the current line of text
Word	CTRL + ←	Left one word at a time
	CTRL + →	Right one word at a time
Paragraph	CTRL + ↑	Up one paragraph at a time
	CTRL + ↓	Down one paragraph
Document	CTRL + HOME	To the beginning of the document
	CTRL + END	To the end of the document
Screen	PAGE UP	Up one full screen
	PAGE DOWN	Down one full screen
Page	CTRL + PAGE UP	To the beginning of the previous page
	CTRL + PAGE DOWN	To the beginning of the next page

APPENDIX III

Keyboard Shortcut tips

The menu shortcut that you learnt in Appendix I will work for these shortcuts by hitting ALT instead of CTRL.

Action	Keyboard Shortcut
Reply	CTRL+R
Reply to everyone	CTRL+SHIFT+R
Create a new item of the same type as the folder you are in	CTRL+N
Mark message as read	CTRL+Q
Switch to viewing by weeks while in Calendar	ALT+HYPHEN
Viewing an open item, you can move to the next item or previous one	CTRL+SHIFT+ → OR CTRL+SHIFT+ ←
Forward	CTRL+F
Switch to your Inbox	CTRL+SHIFT+I
Switch to your Outbox	CTRL+SHIFT+O
Delete	CTRL+D
Remove formatting from selected text	CTRL+SPACEBAR
Select several adjacent items	Click the first item, and then hold down shift and click the last item
Select several non-adjacent items	Click the first item and then hold down ctrl and click each additional item
Select all the items in a folder	Click one of the items and press CTRL+A
Send an open message	ALT+S
Check spelling in an open item	F7
New contact	CTRL+SHIFT+C
New Email	CTRL+SHIFT+M
Advanced Find	CTRL+SHIFT+F

Navigation Pane on and off	ALT+F1
Move between panes in window	F6 (SHIFT+F6 to go backwards)
Move between folders	CTRL+Y
Open a new email	CTRL+SHIFT+M or CTRL+N
Move around fields in a new Email window	TAB (or SHIFT+TAB)
Look up an email address	CTRL+SHIFT+B
Check the validity of an address that you've typed	CTRL+K
Format selected text	Use standard formatting shortcuts, for example, CTRL+B for bold
Open next item	CTRL+COMMA
Open previous item	CTRL+PERIOD
Permanently delete an email	CTRL+DELETE
Move an email	CTRL+SHIFT+V
Create a new folder	CTRL+SHIFT+E

Sample Rules

Brainstorm. Use these ideas as a starting point to dream up rules that are pertinent to you personally and for your business.

1. YOUR PRODUCTIVITY

Create a rule that looks for:

- emails from people NOT in your address book and automatically moves these to a different folder
- emails from a certain email address
- emails on different subjects or committees you belong to and moves them to the appropriate folders
- certain words in the subject line or in the body of the email such as:
  - emails from your friends to go into your 'Friends' folder
  - etickets to go into your 'Travel' folder
  - the word Viagra and have that email go straight to your Deleted Items without ever passing in front of your eyes.

2. WORKING SMARTER

- Have a copy of each email you send go into a folder (in addition to the Sent Items)
- Have the sending of your emails delayed to give you re-think time.

3. JUNK MAIL

- Set a rule to look for specific words in the subject line or in the body of the email and then move the email either to a junk mail folder or delete it
- Set a rule to look for a specific email address (it could be someone that won't take you off their mailing list) and either move it to a junk folder or delete it.

4. MARKETING

Create a rule that:

- tells people when you're out of the office
- moves your incoming emails from product or service providers into their respective folders
- assigns categories to emails
- moves emails into folders by the originating source of enquiry (i.e. Yellow Pages, your website, magazine article, newspaper advertisement)
- puts mail delivery errors into their own folder
- puts newsletter subscribes, unsubscribes and changes of address into their own folders
- forwards certain emails on to someone else to handle
- automatically responds to certain types of emails for you
- uses unique email addresses or pre-coding on your subject lines (Chapter Thirteen) so that:
    - orders that come in from your website or anywhere else go into specific folders
    - website enquires go into an enquiry folder
    - sales enquiries go to a special folder.

    For all three above, you can add a management or overview element by having the original email come in to one person and then forwarding a copy to the correct person to handle – perfect for different sales people handling different products!

Think of the potential for call centres with the combination of incoming emails and rules!

5. ORGANISATIONAL PRIORITY

Have all emails:

- that are not directly addressed to you go into a folder of your choice
- where your name appears in the Cc field go into a 'Cc' folder you create
- where your name appears in the Bcc field go into a 'Bcc' folder you create (Bcc is blind carbon copy)
- coming in from your corporate headquarters go into a 'Headquarters' folder
- coming from HR, or IT, or Admin go into their respective folders
- that are meeting requests or responses go into a separate folder.

6. ORGANISING/CATEGORISING

Have all emails:

- that are newsletters go into your 'Newsletters' folder. Have the rule look for the sender's email address or the name of the newsletter
- have separate newsletter folders for each type of newsletter.

7. AUTORESPONSE:

Create an automatic response when an email is received that:

- requires a standard repetitive response (why do it manually over and over and over again?)
- tells someone you're not in the office or on vacation

- tells someone that you won't get to your emails right away but that you will get back to them.

8. NOTIFICATION

- If important enquires or requests for quotes come in from your website, create a rule to send the email to your mobile phone (if your phone has that capability)
- Let someone know that the individual they're emailing has since left your company.

9. MONITORING STAFF ACTIVITY BY

a. Having email enquiries come in to you.
b. Creating a rule to forward the email on to the staff member responsible for following up.
c. Creating a reporting requirement and then comparing these lists.
d. Have all emails addressed to you stay in your inbox.

Note:

For those with Outlook 2003, don't forget about those wonderful search folders that can work in tandem or instead of rules. Search folders are described in Chapter Three.

Room for your notes as you read